Our Infinite Power to Heal

101 Inspirational Stories of Profound Healing From Within

Emily Gowor & Rae Antony

Dedicated to our father and grandfather, John Antony, for his courage to explore alternative healing in 1959 when it was unheard of to step outside the medical realm for treatment.

Table of Contents

Introduction

1: *Carmen Braga* ....Healing From Anxiety

2: *Amanda Rodd*...A Journey of Healing

3: *Leonie Lancaster*.. The Power Within

4: *Karen Reys* ....Love and Healing

5: *Bridget Wood*.. Finding My Fertility

6: *Shona Blackthorn* ....Guilt Almost Destroyed Me

7: *Daniel Lyttle* .... The Failure That Saved My Life

8: *Louise Cramond*... We Didn't Say Goodbye

9: *Billy Flett*... Finding the Light

10: *Sue McKenna* .... Natural Remedies and Sheer Determination

11: *Kate Moloney* .... Finding Fulfilment from Financial Ruin

12: *Helen Travers*... A Cosmic Awakening

13: *Ayla Saylik*...The Silver Lining

14: *Ana Palacios de las Casas*......................Finding What Was Missing

15: *Anthony Hudson* ....Wake Up and Choose

16: *Irene Treacy* ....Save Others, Save Yourself

17: *Estelita de Cruz Pearce* ....You Are Not Done Yet

18: *Deborah Stathis*... Choice

19: *Heather Joy Bassett* ....An Extremely Extraordinary Woman

20: *Joshua McNess* ....My Body Spoke Up

21: *Emme Krystelle* ....Public Face, Private Face

22: *Delwyn Webb* .... It's a Miracle!

23: *Tami Jane*..Healing in the Fast Lane

24: *Alison Morris* .... A Journey of Self-Empowerment

25: *Jo Tocher*..Life After Miscarriage

26: *Lance Garbutt*.................................... The Wonders of My Mindset

27: *Dr. Marcia Becherel* ....Stepping into Marcia

28: *Maria Solano* .... A Love Letter to Myself

29: *Dannii Orawiec*.....................................There Is Always a Choice

30: *Carolynne Melnyk*.. Where Is My Mom?

31: *Stephan Gardner* ....Beyond Personal Development

32: *Jason Russell*.. From Bullied to Empowered

33: *Jeani Howard*................................My Pure Transformation to Love

34: *Andrea Baumann*.................... On The Rough Road To Redemption

35: *Jeff Withers*..................................... Growing My Soulmate

36: *Fiona Hurle* .... When Life Fails You

37: *Sheila Livingstone* ....Alone, Yet Not Alone

38: *Carolina Rotaru* ....From Misery to Inspiration

39: *Naveen Light* ....Desperation Leads to Discovery

40: *Dave Tuck* ....The Awakening

41: *Elina Passant* ....Seeing Beyond Fear

42: *Heather Passant* ....Fear of Rejection

43: *Delvina Waiti* ....Loving Life Through the Soul

44: *Jo Worthy*.. Heal Your Life

45: *Vas Bes* ....Self-Love Saved My Life

46: *Shaune Clarke*..Let Go of Negative Energies

47: *Jennie de Vine*....................................Healing from Chronic Fatigue

48: *Michelle Walker*...............................Creativity: A Path to Wellness

49: *Helga Dalla* .... Accept and Turn Situations Around

50: *Elysia Anketell*... The Piano

51: *Jackie Mortimer*..The Power of Prayer

52: *Nicole Taryn* .... The Gift of Surrender

53: *Christine Di Leone*..Remembering Mom

54: *Rachel Saliba* ....The Power of Self-Transformation

55: *Nick Condon* ....The Power to Choose

56: *Franca Mazzarella* .... Happily Ever After and Divorced

57: *Anne Namakando Phiri*...........................Against the Cultural Grain

58: *Hilary Cave* .... A Lighter Touch

59: *Robert J Grimes* .... Healing to Freedom and Fullness in Life

60: *Hayley Scott*...Fiercely Determined

61: *Slava Komzic*............................... Confessions of a Personal Trainer

62: *Tony Brown* ....Hope on Hold

63: *Sabrina Souto* ....Conscious Love and Hormones

64: *Kim Guthrie* ....Healing Hashimoto's Through Awareness

65: *Shane Breslin* ....One August Wednesday

66: *Sally Moore*...Overcoming Depression

67: *Maree Malouf*.. Surviving Trauma Through Dance and Relationships

68: *Cat McRad*.. Rebirthed

69: *Katina Cuba* ...... Katina the Peacock Living in the Land of Penguins

70: *Tony Inman* ....From Desperation to Inspiration

71: *Jo Trewartha*.. Lessons in Love

72: *Carlosifus Holden*............................Make Your Choices Right

73: *Hazel Butterworth* .... Finding Me Within

74: *Luanne Mareen* .... My Healing is Their Healing

75: *Angela Peris*... Healing Through the Heart

76: *Natasha Jones* ....Kundalini Rising

77: *Alan Jackson* ....Gut Feeling

78: *Faye Rushton* ....Being Faye

79: *Dr. Olivier Becherel* .... It's Never too Late for Rebirth

80: *Jaswinder Challi Sahiba* ....Through the Flame

81: *Panayiota* ....You Are Your Own Master!

82: *Kim Knight* .... The Day I Saved My Life

83: *Sharyn Bailey* .... The Healing Power of Truth

84: *Faye Waterman* .... Not Seen and Not Heard

85: *Deborah Toussaint* .... Born Broken

86: *George Masempela* .... Overcoming Depression Without Drugs

87: *Manmeet Chowdry* .... Optimum Thinking Works Wonders

88: *Di Riddell* .... Dancing to Different Possibilities

89: *Rachel Gascoine* .... From Toxic to Terrific

90: *Jan McIntyre* .... Growing Bodacious Self-Love

91: *Cindy Galvin* .... The Gift of Being Different

92: *Dr. Kim Jobst* .... Healing from Beyond the Veil

93: *Raelene Byrne* .... Believe In Your Value

94: *Leroy Midgley* .... Be Limitless

95: *Karen Dwyer* .... Responsibility for Oneself

96: *Sigourney Belle Weldon* .... So My Story Begins

97: *Debra White Hughes* .... Healing Cancer Naturally

98: *Laraib Fatima Malik* .... Loving My Life Again

99: *Lee Chapman* .... Five Dollars

100: *Rae Antony* .... Reclaiming My Sleep

101: *Emily Gowor* .... The Healing Power of Writing

Contact the Authors

Recommended Reading

Acknowledgments

About Emily Gowor

About Rae Antony

Introduction

$\mathcal{I}$ first discovered my innate ability to create healing in my body and life at the young age of 17. I was living away from home and completing my final year of school when my first spiritual teacher gave me the book *The Body Is The Barometer Of The Soul* by Annette Noontil.

I soon became fascinated with the process of interpreting the symptoms of my body and understanding the spiritual message they were trying to tell me. It wasn't uncommon for me to stub my toe and run to the book to see what it meant. I had discovered my inner guidance system and developed a deeper relationship with my body: a relationship that I have benefited from immensely.

It was in that same year that I discovered the world of personal development. To cope with my parents' divorce earlier that year and the pressure of suddenly having to look after myself — cooking meals, working a casual job, my final year studies, and more — I read nearly every book on self-help in the Brisbane City Library. I was looking for deeper answers and a way to feel better. During that year and the one that followed, I learnt about creative visualisation, dream interpretation, meditation, neuro-linguistic programming, the power of intention, the subconscious mind, affirmations, and all things to do with spirituality.

I began keeping a day-to-a-page diary. I would write down key learnings each day, including the interpretation of dreams I'd had the night before, messages I'd seen on billboards that gave me the feeling life was talking to me, things people said that had a deeper meaning for me, oracle card interpretations, and more. What I didn't realise at the time was that I was setting an incredibly powerful foundation in place for my future: the ability to tune into and understand oneself in relation to life.

My conviction in the belief that my body, relationships and life were always communicating with me to help me move towards my higher evolution was compounded by every personal breakthrough I experienced along the way. The deep revelations I have encountered, in what has now been more than 12 years of powerful introspection, have guided me through relationship break-ups, the founding of my business, several six-figure revenues, travelling the world, writing and publishing several books, and so much more. My relationship with life gives me the sensation that I am never alone in the world, and has, without a shadow of a doubt, assisted me in connecting with my purpose.

I'm convinced that I truly do have the power to heal myself; and that, when I tap into that power, it is infinite. Miracles can occur, ideas can be born, solutions can appear, and true healing can happen when we begin to look within for the answers to our problems instead of believing that we are at the mercy of what is happening within our bodies, relationships, businesses, and lives. When we seek to awaken from within, the world looks and feels different. Life opens to us, and we begin to see the pathway to do what we love and live a rewarding life instead of one that feels empty and meaningless.

One of the people who I have shared a significant part of this journey of continual awakening with is my mother, Rae Antony (also fondly known as Mama Rae). I have been blessed beyond words to have a relationship with my own mother where we can share and bare all spiritually. I can't count how many deep and profound conversations we have shared where I was 'popped open' by a life-changing epiphany and she has held her heart wide open to witness me in a state of transformation.

These conversations have formed many of the critical turning points on my journey to inspire humanity, and I feel to my core that sharing this journey with her is one of the greatest gifts I can give her. In a way, it is an expression of my gratitude to her for giving me life on this Earth. It has been nothing short of inspiring to watch her on her own journey of self-expansion, and I can say with true and lasting certainty that she has seen my true, authentic self. As I say to people, 'She gets it.'

This is why we have come together to bring this book to life: so that we can open a whole new world for you too, where you realise that you truly do have healing power within you. We believe to our core that when you take your life into your hands, without hesitation, you will access your inner wisdom in a way that will not only inspire but empower you for whatever lies ahead. The 101 stories you are about to read demonstrate this.

You are about to gain a deep insight into the lives and true stories of people who have overcome life-threatening illnesses, divorce, death of loved ones, identity crises, depression, anxiety, bullying, financial adversity and more. Each story shows us that the soul and spirit within each of us cannot be defeated, no matter what we encounter along the way, and there is always hope, no matter how rough the road might seem right now. These stories show us that there are many paths to healing and that we always have a choice in how we respond to the circumstances of our lives.

Our wish is that you will not only be deeply moved as you read this book, but you will feel a sense of faith that regardless of the circumstances you find yourself in – be they personal, professional, physical, or spiritual – you have the ability and the power to grow through it, as these 101 stories show so beautifully. All you need is the courage to look inside yourself and let the light shine through once again.

For whatever challenges you may be facing right now, use these stories as the hope, inspiration, and guiding light that you need on your own healing journey. We created this for you.

With inspiration,

Emily Gowor & Rae Antony

It is important for us to state that we are neither suggesting nor advocating that anyone dismiss the benefits of medical treatment or supplementation for an illness or symptom, as in many cases, medication is an essential aid to the healing process. Our intention is simply to show that there is often another element involved in lasting healing: the restoration of mental and emotional wellbeing.

1

Healing From Anxiety

*J*n 2016, my husband noticed a sore on the side of his tongue that gave him trouble when he ate. After a biopsy, he was diagnosed with tongue cancer. Our world, as we knew it, came to a grinding halt. We felt weak in the knees and our minds were spinning as we wondered, 'What happens now?' We endured seven months of surgery, radiation, feeding tubes, anger, depression, and intense sadness.

Friends and family told me to look after myself, but did I? No! While watching television one day, my heart suddenly started pounding. I was hot and cold at the same time, my ears were ringing, and I was incredibly dizzy! Thinking I was having a heart attack, we rushed to the hospital. We were terrified. After everything we'd been through, the last thing we needed was to end up in the hospital again.

Many tests later, the doctor was stymied. They couldn't find anything wrong with me, so they sent us home. The next day, I got up and felt okay, but around noon, it happened again. Back to the hospital we went. More tests were conducted, each with the same conclusion: there was nothing wrong with me!

I was attended to by a different doctor on my second visit who suggested I was having an anxiety attack, to which I responded, 'What?' This had never happened before. 'How could I have an anxiety attack when I wasn't even doing anything?' I said, rather indignantly. I refused to believe him and was frankly quite upset at the assessment. But guess what? He was right. In retrospect, I had to laugh because the television program we had been watching the day I had my first anxiety attack was on sinkholes. And here I was, in that very moment, sinking into a hole of my own from all the stress I had been through.

Life is full of synchronicities. Right after this happened, I read a passage from one of Eckhart Tolle's books, which said, 'The psychological condition of fear is divorced from any concrete and true immediate danger. It comes in many forms: unease, worry, anxiety, nervousness, tension, dread, phobias, etc. This kind of psychological fear is always in the form of something that 'might' happen, not something that is happening now. You are in the here and now, while your mind is in the future creating this 'imaginary' danger. This creates an anxiety gap. You can cope with the present moment, but you cannot cope with the future 'you' who is creating that imaginary danger.'

This was a huge awakening for me as I realised that the fear I was perpetuating really was psychological. I decided to carry out an experiment. When the next attack occurred, rather than taking a pill, I decided to look within myself instead. I sat down, closed my eyes and took several deep breaths. I then identified what was causing my anxiety at that moment while paying extra attention to the fear I was feeling. Then I asked myself, 'Is this really happening right now?' Of course, the answer was no.

This was amazing, as I got to see firsthand how my anxiety was caused by my overactive imagination! My mind was conjuring up all kinds of scenarios of losing my husband, so naturally I became quite distressed, but none of these things were actually happening. Once I saw this, I was then able to slow my breath down and calm myself to a point of coming back to normal. I only ever had to take the medication prescribed to me twice and it has never happened again. I am grateful for what anxiety has taught me.

Carmen Braga

2

A Journey of Healing

I was diagnosed with Crohn's disease just a week after getting engaged. What I dreamed would be the most joyful and exciting time of my life turned into the most challenging. In the middle of trying on wedding dresses, organising a reception venue, and booking a photographer, I was in and out of hospital. After trialling countless medications with little relief, I had bowel surgery.

Crohn's disease is an autoimmune disorder that causes inflammation in the digestive tract which leads to diarrhea, blood in the stools, abdominal pain, fatigue, and malnutrition. It can have serious complications like fistulas (an abnormal passageway between two organs, or an organ and the skin) and perforation of the bowel.

At the height of my flares, I was opening my bowels up to 20 times a day. The toilet bowl would fill with blood and I would be in constant pain; a pain much worse than childbirth. I would open my eyes every morning and wonder how I was going to get through another day of unimaginable emotional and physical pain. One morning, I remember thinking to myself, 'I can't do this anymore.'

During one of the countless hospital stays, I sat by the window and started admiring the trees outside. I watched the way they bent with the wind, flowing with the breeze, not against it. There was no struggle as they allowed themselves to lean into what was around them.

I thought to myself, 'What if I stop resisting my experience and stop pushing against my body? What might happen if I start to embrace my reality and look for the opportunities in front of me?' That was the moment I decided to consciously heal my body.

I began a practice of gratitude that would see me heal both emotionally and physically. I started to appreciate all that was well in my body. I was thankful for my senses, for my limbs that were in perfect working order and my strong heart. I started to appreciate my brain, my intelligence, and the way my body took a breath and gave me life with total automaticity.

Once I moved from feeling despair to hope, I began researching the connection between our emotions and the physical symptoms we experience. I realised that I had manifested Crohn's disease by engaging in negative self-talk and self-criticism. I was suppressing my emotions and keeping myself busy with two jobs, pretending that I was fine on the outside when I was hurting on the inside. I took full responsibility for where I was in life. I forgave myself and healed my emotional torment to experience physical healing.

Although I live with Crohn's today, my symptoms are now manageable. I love knowing that life is happening for me, not to me, and I look for the blessings that are found in the challenges I experience. I am now able to work full-time doing a job that I love. I have three beautiful children with my husband who stuck by me and was the rock by my side through it all. Instead of wondering how I am going to get through the day, I now wake up each morning excited and full of joy that I get to live this magnificent life that I have created.

Being diagnosed with Crohn's disease was the most challenging experience of my life, but it would turn into the biggest gift life could give me.

Amanda Rodd

3

The Power Within

*H*aving been a health practitioner for 25 years, I began a two-year post-graduate course in functional neurology in 2013. It was hectic, but I craved knowledge and was willing to make any sacrifices needed to achieve my goal. I turned every spare moment into a study opportunity, ignoring the instinctual need to take a break. I resisted listening to what my body needed, and I kept pushing myself. The academic endeavour had become all-consuming; I felt an inner turmoil but was helpless to do anything about it.

Leading into the exams, a strange thing was happening. The more I studied different neurological symptoms, the more I felt like I had them myself. Surely not? Maybe I was just overtired and after the exams finished, all the weird stuff that was happening to me would just disappear. So, I kept ignoring the reality of what was going on and focused my attention on the overwhelming mountain of textbooks in front of me.

By the time exam results were out, my neurological dysfunctions were impacting me more. Walking was difficult as I kept falling to my left side and dragging my right foot. My tongue felt heavy, making it difficult to speak. There were all sorts of numbness, itchiness and dizziness, and I felt my vision kept changing.

All this seemed so bizarre that I felt I could not talk to anyone about it. Nothing made sense. I guess I was still hoping that it would magically go away. There was a part of me that thought it could not possibly be real, and another that was too scared to be told a diagnosis. So, I tried to diagnose myself.

Now, I was not only frustrated at my condition, but at being incapable of diagnosing myself. So, I retreated into my study room. Being alone seemed so much easier. Even though I was still incredibly tired, sleep was difficult as thoughts of the potential diagnosis swirled around in my mind. Then, one night, in a moment of clarity, I just knew it was

Multiple Sclerosis (MS). The very moment I realised it, there was an incredible feeling of peace. A voice deep inside me said, 'You're okay.' I immediately fell into a restful and much-needed sleep, and awoke the next day instinctively knowing that everything was going to be okay.

I was still extremely unwell, but after that moment of clarity, everything changed. The burden of fatigue I had resented now seemed to give me the opportunity to sit quietly and be present with myself. I had previously become anxious about this isolation, as I felt so disconnected from the world. But now I realised that in this space I was afforded the opportunity to deeply contemplate my inner voice and learn to trust it, increase my certainty through quiet knowing, find my truth, and discover the spark within me.

A brain MRI confirmed my self-diagnosis. Seeing all the lesions in my brain was a strange experience. For so long, I had been trying to ignore what my body was telling me, and here it was in black and white. Previously, I had been desperately ignoring the signals my body was sending me, and now here I was with swathes of numbness throughout, wishing that I could feel the signals. The irony of that is not lost on me. I know to listen. More importantly, I know how.

When I think of the wisdom that sits inside us, and the amazing capacities our bodies have, I feel immensely humble and appreciative. MS gave me the essential reminder that healing comes from within. I still love to study and gain knowledge about health, but I can now integrate that with the innate wisdom of our bodies.

Leonie Lancaster

4

Love and Healing

"*Y*ou are floundering. Aren't you?" said Uncle Edgar, an Australian Indigenous Traditional Healer. I cried uncontrollably as I retraced the events in my life that had led to my feeling of being dis-empowered, belittled, frustrated, angry, unheard, and debilitated. I asked him to help me heal. "I don't want to feel this way anymore. I don't want to be this person. How can you help me?" I asked.

My supportive parents taught us the importance of being honest, trustworthy, and responsible and raised us to be 'better than we were' because of our experiences of racial discrimination. It was to help protect us in a 'white man's world.' "If you can't talk properly, don't talk at all!" Dad said. This pressure and my learning disability meant that my journey was going to be a challenge.

As an adult, there were many situations in my career when I had allowed myself to be traumatised. I couldn't understand how a person could be so hurtful and harmful. Why were changes not made to a situation at work that affected the health of myself and others? I couldn't articulate my experiences. I just kept retelling the incidents as they had happened. I was determined to understand what I had been through with the office bully and to stand up against the injustice.

As a result, I was diagnosed with Post-Traumatic Stress Disorder. It affected my career, finances, family, relationships, and my sense of self worth for over seven years. I knew the time had come to walk away. I remember sitting at my desk. I couldn't work. I was numb. There was nothing more that I could do. I had done my best. After I resigned, I spiralled downwards. It felt like my whole world had been taken away for the second time and I was reliving the loss of my daughter.

I hadn't slept. I hadn't eaten. I was in a stupor. "I hear you calling me, Ancient Mother. I hear your song". I chanted as the pile of artworks grew larger: I intuitively connected the words, from the song *Ancient Mother* to my artworks that I was now throwing into a heap on the floor.

I was delusional. I believed that evil spirits were trapped in the paintings. I called John, a colleague, to come to our house and to take ownership of the Aboriginal artworks. Instead of taking them away, John listened as I cried, replaying the unjust occurrences for hours. When he left, I felt so embarrassed. I sat still.

The stillness had triggered an unforeseen journey towards healing that was calling me home to 'country,' to my ancestral lands to heal and to be a healer. It was the first time that I had truly felt heard. In that moment of understanding, I had a spiritual awakening. It began a process of automatic writing. The poems about love and forgiveness came from my dad in heaven. I later realised the effect of the self-defeating mantra that I had internalised since childhood.

Uncle's traditional healing ceremony had led me to appreciate my past and to find my purpose in life, as a healer. When I trust myself and face my fears, my voice gets stronger. I have this innate ability to listen deeply: to express myself uniquely and create a safe space for teaching and learning. This is my gift to the world.

It was many years later that I came face to face with the office bully again. I no longer felt the pain in my heart. I didn't need to retell the story. I had forgiven. I give thanks for the healing.

Karen Reys

5

Finding My Fertility

*D*uring my first pregnancy, I felt the most feminine and confident in my body that I had ever felt in my life. Years of natural therapies to treat PCOS (polycystic ovary syndrome), a devastating miscarriage, and consequently, an intentional journey to become a mother, led me to find myself rather than lose myself amongst the challenges of trying to give birth.

The birth of my child was an awakening. As I settled into my role as a mother, my child reflected back to me my own unhealed childhood wounds. It was overwhelming at times. Was it 'enough' if I identified myself primarily as a mother on a path to consciously parent her son? I wondered when would we expand our family further.

As we celebrated his first birthday, and then his second, with no sign of my fertility returning, I was very reluctant to settle into the label of 'secondary infertility', having traversed the dogma of Western medicine once before.

So, I tried healing with food, balancing my hormones by cutting out sugar, wheat and all toxins from my environment. I began nourishing myself with herbs, acupuncture, and chiropractic care. Still, the elephant in the room lingered. I was not yet ready to face it.

My insatiable desire to expand my family and myself through motherhood finally led me to reluctantly examine the beliefs and stories I held about myself not being enough as a woman and thus needing approval to let go of control and step up into my dreams. It was illuminating. I was inspired to share my message with the world through building a community and a business.

But I still felt like my fertility was missing. I knew there was a daughter waiting for me. I just had to get out of my own way. The teacher that I knew could help me do just that was Dr. John Demartini. Studying and applying his work had transformed my outlook on the world, and I knew it could change how I viewed myself, too. At his signature program, The Breakthrough Experience®, I spent a day transforming the judgement I had on myself as 'not fertile.' I looked for all the areas in my life and my body to see where I was fertile. Like all energy, nothing is missing, it's conserved; we just have to learn where to look. As facilitators helped me break down my walls of resistance, I found it. I cried healing tears. The vitality in my body returned, and once again I had certainty that my baby would come in her own time, in our time.

Two months later, while preparing to speak on stage in front of 700 people to launch my podcast, *Nourishing the Mother*, which focuses on intentional mothering, expansion, and awakening the feminine, my period returned. I couldn't quite believe it. And then I realized that I actually could because I was doing the work. I was transforming my story and integrating my wholeness, rather than focusing on the thing I felt was most painfully missing.

The podcast became a form of therapy for my co-host and me, as well as our listeners. It charts the highs and lows, expansion, and contraction that the motherhood journey brings. In episode 34, I announced that I was finally pregnant again with my dreamed-of daughter. Sylvie was born one year later, to the day, after I stood on that stage and spoke of the wisdom, value, and reverence we must have for ourselves as mothers.

Bridget Wood

6

Guilt Almost Destroyed Me

"*I* can't live without you." I had heard my husband say this many times over the years.

He had been diagnosed with bipolar disorder 15 years earlier. With his changing moods, I never knew what to expect next. Staying was traumatic, yet leaving was unthinkable. I thought I was doing the right thing. Now, when I look back in hindsight, I realise I wasn't. The children didn't know their father had a mental disorder.

On a visit to the psychiatrist, I was asked to stay back on the pretence of receiving an update on my husband's medication. That day, life changed for me forever. He warned me that my husband was approaching a complete mental collapse and, if this happened, he would not only take his own life but also take my life and our children's. Terror struck me. We were in grave danger. I had to make a plan to escape.

I told my children that we were leaving their father. My heart was breaking for them, but I had to be strong, for there was no turning back. We became short of money and it wasn't long before we moved in with a friend. It was only a two-bedroom unit, but this would have to do for the time being.

I was terrified that my husband would find us. One night when the doorbell rang, my greatest fear was realised. I opened the door and he was standing there. It was about eight o'clock on a Saturday evening. I could tell he had had a complete breakdown. He wanted me to go home with him, but I refused. I knew what was in store for me and my family if I did. I found out the next day when the police arrived that he had finally carried out his threat and taken his own life.

That's when I started drinking. I would have gone insane without it. I eventually found a large house for us and did what I could to keep my family together. The children were my world. There were many nights where I couldn't stand up, and my son would put me to bed. Other nights, I would get in the car and drive aimlessly. I was a mess. Guilt was torturing me. Was it my fault the children lost their father? Should I have stayed? Drinking was the only way to numb the guilt I felt.

For two years, I drank every day, trying to stop, but failing. Then something happened. I woke up one morning, and I felt a sudden change in me. What happened overnight was like a miracle. I knew it was time to change, and I did. I stopped drinking and turned my life around. It was hard. It took a lot of soul-searching, but I did it.

I found myself again. I had the motivation to climb out of the hole I had dug for myself. I was ready to set goals. They were small ones to start with and then I aimed for bigger and better ones. First, I had to find a job. I was offered a position with a weight-loss company as a consultant, and within six months, I was promoted to manager. After two years, I became a Recruitment Officer.

My past has led me to where I am today: A Certified Hypnotherapist, Counsellor, and published co-author. I am currently writing my first novel and I hope it won't be my last. I have a fire burning in my soul and nothing will stop me from achieving whatever I put my mind to.

What would have happened if I hadn't had that moment of sudden healing when I stopped drinking? Where would we be now? I know that I am one of the lucky ones.

Shona Blackthorn

7

The Failure That Saved My Life

2011 was shaping up to be an amazing year. My income was growing, my clients loved me, I was making a name in the industry. I was giving back to the community, and I had just proposed to my girlfriend. As a philanthropic entrepreneur, I had made it. Then, after a messy split from my business partner, the business and I took a heavy hit. Income dried up, bills started to rise, and so did the stress. I knuckled down: I was not afraid of hard work. The engine was revving, the wheels were spinning, but I was still moving slowly. Friends, clients and associates were affected. I was embarrassed and depressed.

As a typical male, I devoted every waking hour to my struggling passion. This put strain on my relationship as I wondered, 'Why can't she understand I'm doing this for us?' I needed my wife-to-be to respect my business needs, not realising I was neglecting hers. The next nine months were hell. I was heavily in debt, newly single, lonely, and fighting to stay out of bankruptcy. My perfect world had collapsed. The clients whom I had seen as family no longer wanted to speak to me, and the only calls I got were from debt collectors and banks.

It was all too much. I'd had enough. I'd failed at everything! I even tried taking my own life, but I failed at that too when the rope broke. I had hit rock bottom. I remember thinking that if I found something funny to watch on YouTube, maybe it would help cheer me up.

The first thing on my newsfeed was a video from a personal trainer in the USA titled, 'Why suicide is a silly idea'. I know how crazy that sounds. He said, "Life is full of seasons. If you hate winter, don't despair, it's always followed by spring and summer. Tough times will always pass." He shared other videos about releasing depression through vibration and bioresonance. I knew about *chi* and loved the idea. What I learnt that day has forever changed my life as a person and as a practitioner. I accepted that life is full of seasons, winter will not last forever and neither will summer. I also learnt how to pull myself back up faster. Sure, downs will happen, just don't let them become too deep or too long.

This is how I changed my vibration and saved my life: I jumped, bounced and moved every part of my body randomly and sporadically, whilst humming and chanting in a deep voice. I let it all jiggle and flop about uncontrollably, letting my arms flail and landing flat-footed so the thump of my heel reverberated up my body. I was liberating and vibrating every single cell from its neurotic holding pattern.

It felt silly to begin with, but when done right, I began resonating on a new level. For one of many reasons—including poor nutrition, lack of movement, illness, disease or chemical imbalance—your vibration may be lower than normal. Using this technique, you can increase your vibration and give yourself a pick-up. The effects don't last forever, because the body is dynamic and constantly evolving, but add it to your daily or weekly routine and watch your life change.

My life isn't perfect. I still struggle with depression and have had tough times. It's a part of life. But, if you learn the tools to empower yourself, and improve how you treat, talk to, and love yourself, life will be significantly easier.

Be good to yourself: you two will be together for a while.

Daniel Lyttle

8

We Didn't Say Goodbye

When Maurice passed away, I was left hollow and numb with gut-wrenching grief. I was haunted with unhealed experiences from our past, lingering pauses of unfinished sentences, so many words desperate to be said, and the unbelievable loss to our three children. But most of all, I felt the anguish of not having had the chance to say goodbye, which tormented every part of my being.

Consumed with pain and sorrow I wondered how I would ever heal. Most nights I would journal and try to meditate to settle my mind and the anxiousness in my body. One evening, six months after Maurice had passed away, I went to bed exhausted and needing to write down my thoughts.

As I was journaling, I was overtaken by a tidal wave of emotion and intense pain in my chest and abdomen so powerful I threw myself out of bed, falling to my knees. I was taken by surprise. From deep down within my belly came a scream so primal and full of anguish. "Where are you?" I cried, "Can you hear me?" I slumped to the floor and sobbed until there was nothing left inside me.

In the morning, I was woken softly by the dance of the sun on my face. Adjusting my body in bed, I recalled a dream I had just had where Maurice and I had said goodbye to each other. I went to write down my dream so that I wouldn't forget it. But instead, I wrote: 'Maurice, goodbye my darling, it's not the end. There is not a moment that I don't think of you. All our problems seem so obsolete now. All I feel is our love. Please talk to me. I just want to hear your voice. I do believe we can communicate, but I'm not sure how.'

Closing my eyes more words came as I dropped into stillness. Listening I heard a voice and froze too scared to move. It was Maurice.

'There is no gap between us; we are one. Our minds are linked. There will always be communion with me, for we are one. We always have been, you just didn't know it.'

'It's so tricky. My logical mind is trying to work this out.'

'You always did too much of that. It made me feel insecure in my earthly illusion.'

'My pain is my barrier to you, Maurice. We let our pain stop so much. We pulled down the shutters to the love that is always there. I want to open my heart. I feel I have had it locked up for so long.'

'Yes, we brought that out in each other. But it was our own closed hearts that we didn't see. We blamed one another's closed heart.'

'Why didn't I see this sooner?'

'You weren't meant to.'

'Why did you have to go now? We were just beginning to understand.'

'It's not the end. No blame. We are doing it now, aren't we? We are going to open our hearts now. Love is all there is.'

'Why didn't we do this before?'

'We are doing it now.'

As I closed my eyes, tears of joy ran down my face and I allowed myself to feel pure love. These writings, and those that followed, opened the doorway to a profound healing of my heart, mind, and spirit. I soon discovered my journey with spiritual writing and the gradual awakening to the truth of who I AM.

Louise Cramond

9

Finding the Light

From the time I was a teenager until my mid 30s, mania and depression tainted my world. Depression was a dark cloud descending; my mind was scattered and heavy. I found it hard to function or even working out what to wear or eat. I lost hope, jobs, and my passion for life. This could last for months.

Then I would look after myself with good food and exercise and my life would get back on track. This too would last for a few months before the mania inevitably returned. The episodes progressively worsened as the years went by. I didn't know any different, that was me and that was how I rolled through life, up and down to the extremes! All I wanted was to find the underlying reason and heal, to end this waking nightmare.

Over the years, I tried many different natural therapies and experienced temporary relief. When I was unable to cope, I went on anti-depressants. Then at 30 years old, I was diagnosed with bipolar disorder. I was so headstrong and determined to heal myself naturally that I refused to take the prescribed medication. Deep down, I knew there was another way and I knew I would find it, one day.

I researched, studied and practised alternate therapies and self-healing, including Reiki and NLP. Yet I still swung back to my old dysfunctional manic and depressive life. Under the guidance of a naturopath, I went on a strict diet, including multiple supplements. Over time, I became balanced and physically well, however, I found the diet hard to maintain and very expensive. I fell back into my old ways and the mania returned, my life went out of control again, followed by the deep crash into depression.

In 2011, I found myself in the familiar pattern and had no choice but to go on medication again. This enabled me to get back on my feet and provided a stable mind and the space to find a cure. I was not content, I had gained a lot of weight due to the medication, I was unwell, yet stable, purely existing day to day with no drive or passion for life or any of my creative pursuits or dreams. Something had to change. I was shocked by the huge A-Z list of pharmaceuticals on offer that all masked the cause of bipolarism. I was drawn to a herbal supplement that relieved the symptoms of bipolar, ADD, and OCD. Whilst taking the herbs, I slowly went off the medication and experienced no mania or depression.

I did a spiritual development course, for which my intention was to find more love and peace in my life. Yet I found so much more. By releasing stored emotions and stories, I allowed more light and love to reside within me. By expanding my love of self, I found a new way of life. As I moved through my old suppressed emotions, beliefs, perception, and concepts, my life changed. Although challenging at times, it was absolutely worth it!

I began to find myself again, I looked after myself well, I lost 40 kilograms, my thyroid problems cleared as did the sleep apnoea I was experiencing. My dreams, desires, and goals returned. I found and am still finding more love of self; experiencing more peace and joy and wonder in this magical world we live.

It took two decades of mental madness and determination to find the answer. The solution I found is simply loving self, through letting go of the old that no longer serves you allowing you to find more love of self. Since 2015 I have lived a stable, contented, and grounded life. At times the journey has not been easy, yet I wouldn't have it any other way.

Billy Flett

10

Natural Remedies and Sheer Determination

*M*y mother died of breast cancer, and so I developed a strong desire to keep my body and mind in excellent condition. I always had lots of energy, and I was healthy and optimistic. I rarely felt sick or debilitated. But then I felt a lump in my breast in 2010. In 2012, I felt another lump. An ultrasound and biopsy revealed three lumps, the largest being a m ductal carcinoma. The doctors suggested mastectomy, chemotherapy and tamoxifen for five years.

That night, while soaking in a hot bath, crying and thinking of my two sons losing their mum, I realised that, as I had always flown the flag for natural healing, this was my opportunity to walk my talk, get on, and do it. With absolute determination and a belief that my body is a self-healing mechanism capable of reabsorbing the lumps, I opened my mind, heart, and soul to the universe to guide me.

I searched online, went to the health shops, booked time with healers. I knew it could be done. I felt excited though I didn't know how I was going to pay for it all. The healers and supplements were expensive. The community organised raffles and fundraisers to aid me. People came up to me in the street and handed me money. I was taken aback at people's generosity and am deeply thankful.

I went on a 28-day vegetable juice and broth cleanse with rest and sleep. I took vitamin and mineral tablets. Realising that they were mostly synthetic, I substituted 'real' foods and herbs, which proved more effective with less strain on my body. I used turmeric, garlic, coconut oil, cinnamon, cayenne, and fresh herbs from the garden. I also ate superfoods such as goji, cacao, seaweed, blueberries, kimchi, miso, natural yoghurt, and other fermented foods.

After the cleanse, I stayed on juices and raw foods for several months. I began to feel depleted. Blood tests showed I was deficient in B12, iron, vitamin D, protein, and fats. Not only this, I had adrenal fatigue and leaky gut. I began having organic beef bone broths, liver, cod liver oil, cooked and steamed vegetables, and lots of butter – phew! I drank herbal teas such as the essiac formula, cat's claw, pau d'arco, slippery elm, astragalus, ginger, licorice, burdock root and dandelion. I used intravenous laetrile (B17) and medicinal cannabis oil.

I applied black salve, and I took the tincture for 6 months. One of the lumps extraordinarily popped out! Two lumps still to go! I made a balm with coconut oil, hemp seed oil, Lugol's iodine, magnesium oil, and therapeutic grade essential oils, which I massaged into my breasts twice daily. I did Reiki and visualised daily, constantly reaffirming that I was already healed. I walked, danced, stretched, had hot baths with magnesium salts and essential oils, skin brushed, rested, and slept regularly.

Within six months, I felt fitter. All tests showed improvement. I was also going through menopause, so I took supplements and herbs to help my hormones. This was, after all, considered a hormonal cancer, so it was imperative to support my endocrine system. I had an ultrasound every three months. A year after I began my regime, the remaining two had disappeared. It feels like everything I did made them benign, which then allowed my body to clean up the rest.

I now enjoy the best of health, caring for, and nourishing myself and living my dreams. I am fully myself, giving, and receiving love and respect with everyone I meet and all that I do. I have been clear for over six years.

Sue McKenna

11

Finding Fulfilment from Financial Ruin

J started saving money at age 9. I had made several financial investments by the time I was 19, including buying my first home. I rapidly paid down the mortgage. Creating wealth inspired me.

To accelerate my progress, I attended property seminars. I loved learning. However, due to my naivety and infatuation with my mentors; I lost my sense of self and became hungry to 'get-rich-quick'. To increase my income and buy more investment properties, I moved to a mining town called Moranbah and drove dump trucks. I had two lives: one where I was inspired by my property investing, and another where I was miserable. By age 24, I owned 20 investment properties and had won the Australian Property Investor of the Year Award. It was inspiring to be a high achiever; however, I was $6 million in debt and had invested using very high-risk strategies.

I quit work and travelled the world for six months with my husband, thinking we would move to the Sunshine Coast in Australia and become full-time property investors. Then the property market started to crash. It fell more than 80% in three years. The day I realised that if we sold our entire portfolio we would still have millions of dollars of debt was heartbreaking. I was depressed, fearful, ashamed, and anxious. I was at my lowest point. I collapsed on the floor. I couldn't breathe, my body went numb, and I wanted to leave the planet. In that same moment, a voice in my head said, 'You need to work with a life coach.'

My emotional healing took three years of consistent work with several coaches. I was deeply challenged by the thing I loved: wealth creation. In 3.5 years, we went from having $920,000 in equity to selling everything and still having $4.62+ million debt. Part of my recovery meant returning to Moranbah to clean up our financial mess. As we drove there, between tears, these words just fell out of my mouth: "One day we will come out of this, unscarred and our financial losses will seem as insignificant as losing $1 today." A deep part of me knew that life had bigger plans for us, provided we showed up and dealt with our challenges.

Recovering wasn't easy. There was a lot of work to do: selling all our properties in depressed markets, communicating with all parties involved, repairing my health and marriage, healing shame and balancing my emotional state. Life quickly shifted when I started seeing the big-picture benefits of our financial challenges and how they were serving others as well as myself. I started treating the situation like a university rather than an event to begrudge.

Three years after moving back to Moranbah, I was given an opportunity to move to and work in Brisbane. I thought that losing millions of dollars would end my career in business, yet it had enhanced it. Failure should never be taken personally, because you can't fail unless you've already succeeded at something. Today, I am incredibly grateful to have faced such massive challenges, as they have made me wiser and more resilient. I trust myself above others. I am the one in charge of my financial destiny.

My relationship with money has been transformed. I have systems and rituals around tracking, measuring, and managing it. I am more patient with money because I have created a life that I don't need to escape from. Wealth creation is not just about managing, growing, and investing money, it's also about mastering your emotions, being flexible in your thinking, and having the patience to stick with your long-term version, no matter what challenges you face.

Kate Moloney

12

A Cosmic Awakening

*J*n 1996, on a warm Sunday afternoon at the Mevlana Meditation Centre in St Kilda, Melbourne, Australia, 18 people were about to receive attunements, a kind of symbolic induction into the healing art of Reiki. I'd been breaking out in coughing fits after paying the deposit six weeks prior, continuing right up to the event.

"Barking at the world,' someone in the class said, 'What is it you want to say?" Geez, where do I start? I had been 17 years in rebellion from an ultraconservative religion that preaches the coming of Armageddon and the end of the world. I still believed, that because I had lived recklessly and treacherously, I was condemned to die any day. The result? PTSD and chronic fatigue. It felt like I was peering at the world through gauze. I didn't want people getting close to me.

A couple of friends had suggested I try learning Reiki to, as they put it, "help tune into your inner voice and inner healing capacities". It would involve laying hands on me, which sounded demonic. Had an evil spirit already been trying to strangle me for the last six weeks? Don't laugh! Many people in the world believe this too. What the hell?! I was 37 and desperate to find a way out of this funk.

As we practised on one another over the weekend, I realised just how warm and caring the people around me were. Not only that, I fully experienced how gentle and nurturing Reiki felt. At 3:00 p.m., attunement sessions began. I had a cough drop stuffed inside each of my cheeks. We sat on chairs and closed our eyes. Alison's dress swished as she walked around us. I wondered idly if she was so bored that she was looking at the ceiling while wandering around the room, waving and shaking things.

She stopped in front of me, gently placing her hands on my head. It felt nice. My feet tingled. Then, like a tsunami, tingling surged up through my legs and through my entire body. "Bless you, Alison. God bless you." I began sobbing. Alison kneeled and took my hands. I kissed them. "Bless you, oh God bless you. Thank you." I was like a novice nun kissing the hands of a Mother Superior. This would be considered demonic speech where I came from. Yet I felt something deep inside of myself releasing. Afterwards, some of the class asked if I'd had a revelation. "No," I shrugged, "I just became very emotional suddenly."

Walking home at the end of the day, I felt light and happy for the first time in almost 18 years. It was as though something had reached into the inner depths of my psyche. Two and a half days later, the cough disappeared completely.

In the weeks that followed, for the first time in my life, I was able to meditate regularly with deeply personal insights. People remarked how they'd never seen me look so serene. I was glowing. "Are you in love?" they would ask me. 'No,' I'd tell them, "It was just something that came over me during the final day of Reiki." It was like my heart and mind opened for the first time in my life. Instead of waking each day feeling tired and pointless, there was optimism. A creative part of myself that had been buried since childhood began to emerge. Four months later, I fell in love!

A synchronicity of fantastic events continued to transform my outlook. Never again would I feel unworthy of being alive. While some health problems took a few more years to overcome, never again would I allow the teachings of any religion control my life. I had found personal freedom.

Helen Travers

13

The Silver Lining

I have always been so intrigued and captivated by personal development. I loved learning about the mind and the spiritual force that binds us all together. Eventually, I studied counselling and found myself working with organisations that dealt with individuals who were in crisis and in need of emotional relief. I remember learning about the Law of Attraction and, as a result, I was able to co-create the experience of getting married and starting a family.

What occurred after fulfilling this lifelong desire was something that changed me forever. My husband turned to drug use to deal with his afflictions and things quickly spiralled downhill in my life. I was in crisis and despair, and I now had a young child to care for. It was no longer about me or the people I worked with, it was about having to use all the processes and teachings I had grasped over the years and really make a choice.

I remember being on my knees after much heartache and destruction. I only had two options: end my life or continue living. The choice was easy—I had my child who needed me. However, that meant living in constant terror, fear, anxiety, and uncertainty. This was not good enough. I could not possibly continue living this way. I had absolutely no control over the destruction that was occurring around me. I was immersed in the depths of trauma and despair, and there was nothing I could do externally to make it better.

Throughout all the books I had read, I was always intrigued by the words: 'You create your own reality.' I started to question this deeply. I became angry with myself at a result, because if this were true—and every part of me resonated with this statement—then why had I created such profound destruction in my reality? I concluded that I had failed at life. This belief did not serve me, as it caused even more anguish and despair, so once again I had to dig deep and make another choice.

This time my choice involved taking responsibility for and ownership of everything that was occurring around me. I decided that I must start where I am and question all the beliefs and judgements that I had suppressed about myself. I spent days and nights unravelling them all. At the time I had no idea that this process would lead to the amazing life I now live.

I was motivated every moment of the day to continuing this process. I went into the places of my own buried hurt and trauma that I had kept myself from facing for many years. I had masked these feelings with desires outside of myself rather than looking within, because it gave me relief from the despair and emotional pain I was feeling. It was the only thing I could control.

What occurred by simply trusting this process created a ripple effect in my external world. My husband, who I was separated from at the time, started mirroring me. He started reflecting all the love, compassion and worthiness I was showing myself. He fully recovered from his drug addiction and the three of us became a family once again, which was what my heart desired. I began to simply let go of that which I couldn't control and focus on what I could (my feelings). I truly thank my husband, because it is through the challenges he faced that I was able to transform my life by healing myself within, which is something I continue to do as a daily practice.

Ayla Saylik

14

Finding What Was Missing

*L*ike almost everyone, I have been searching for something special, like an amazing gift or a great treasure, that could give me the magical key to find the path of happiness and to open up the completeness of the perfect human being inside me. In this search, I focused on what was missing in me. For many years, I pondered this question. I felt incomplete. I was not married and did not have children. This made me feel that I was not good enough and this perception froze my heart. I lived in fear and anxiety, which manifested itself in panic attacks twice a day for almost four years.

I decided not to use medication for the anxiety and to try only natural ways and psychology. My body and mind suffered because these options worked very slowly. Each day, when I went outside my secure zone – my home and neighbourhood – to go to work, or shopping, or do any simple thing, the sensation of vulnerability and not being able to manage the deep fear and panic was disabling.

I lost my self-esteem, and the need for 'external acceptance' guided me towards the abandonment of my own being, myself, and my individuality. My life was like a ship without a rudder. I was ready to please others but not to listen to myself. I was afraid to show my vulnerability, and that emotion locked me up in a jail, not with bars, but with the limitation to the freedom that I imposed on myself. Time went by and this thought plagued my mind.

My desperation increased, and I cried to God for help. And here is the best part: when you search or ask God, or the universe, or whatever you call it, for guidance in your journey, you will always receive an answer. In 2011, two years before my 50th birthday, while watching a TV program, I heard about a book titled *The Four Agreements*, written by Don Miguel Ruiz, a Mexican spiritual teacher.

The statements were very impressive. I decided to read it and put it into practice. They were extremely liberating, and I consider that to be the first step in my life transformation. Taking my first steps down this path was like being a baby again but I felt I could face this challenge, like any event in my life. Once again, I already had the support I needed, because we are never alone even if the circumstances may seem that way.

It was amazing how the information and people, which could give me the guidance to change my mind, appeared. I started believing in myself and feeling I deserved my heart's desires. It was magical because my physical appearance changed, too. I discovered that I was complete and that nothing was missing inside me. My essence was like the essence of everybody. This feeling gave me life.

I understood that if I did not accept myself and what I am, external approval and acceptance would not arrive. I did not need to receive it from others; rather, I needed to accept my own essence. What is missing is what you are not giving to yourself. Once I started to accept myself for who I am – with my strengths and weaknesses and my own uniqueness – I found my authentic self.

Love must start with oneself. When you listen to your heart and experience the greatness of love – not only romantic love but also compassionate and unconditional love – miracles happen. The miracle happens because love is healing and creative. It expands, nourishes, delivers and enlightens. This experience has been like a rebirth to me. Every day we can become reborn and have second chances to manifest the power of love.

Ana Palacios de las Casas

15

Wake Up and Choose

I was at university sitting in a lecture for my degree in Engineering and I fell asleep – again. It did not matter how much I slept, what I ate or how much I exercised, it always felt as if I hadn't slept for days.

I went to the doctor and explained my condition. At first, his response was, It is university, everyone sleeps, try x, then y. I followed his advice, but nothing changed. Then, I had several blood tests to see what was happening. Everything kept coming back clear. I remember feeling like I was crazy and that the doctors were incapable of helping me. I couldn't believe they were unable to find what was wrong with me. Eventually I was referred to a specialist and, after a sleep test, it was discovered I had narcolepsy. To the doctor's surprise, my reaction was one of excitement. Someone finally had an answer and a diagnosis. They put me on drugs and my health improved.

The drugs worked for a little while and my condition improved, but after a couple of years, things began to worsen and more symptoms appeared. No longer was it just a sleeping problem, it felt like my body was shutting down. I remember some days it felt like I was walking through mud. Just talking to people required so much thought and effort that it resulted in a headache. One day, while at work, I yelled, "There's a fire!" only to discover I was the only one seeing the smoke.

I could see that things were getting worse. I thought there had to be something more to the doctor's diagnosis that no one knew about. I returned to the specialist and shared my experience and my thoughts about the health issues I was facing. He asked me, "Would you consider that it might be psychological?" I was stunned. Psychological? How could my mind be causing all these physical symptoms? Lumps, sleep issues, speech impairment? This sounded absurd! However, I took it on. I was willing to try anything to get off the drugs and avoid a more serious health complication.

I went to a psychologist. I explained to him the experience of having tingles in my left hand. He asked what it meant to me. I explained that it was another piece of evidence that something was seriously wrong with me. He asked, "What if you made it mean something else?" I stopped, surprised and confused. He went on to ask, "Why don't you make it mean that you are stressed, or haven't had enough water, or eaten the right food. It could be anything. Who knows? Experiment."

The next day the tingles started again. I looked down at my hand and made a choice. I chose to make it mean stress. I looked at what might be causing stress, and, in that moment, the most profound thing happened: the tingles disappeared! This was the turning point in my health and life. My mental state had influenced my physical state. It was like my body was sending me a message and when I received the message, my body relaxed. From that point onwards, I began to listen to my body in a different way. I now understand that my body was not attacking me, it was guiding me.

I no longer have narcolepsy. As an engineer, life coach, and spiritual healer, I have committed my life to causing a paradigm shift in the way the world looks at and treats illness and diseases so that others can live their purpose without constraints. I have explored a variety of healing modalities on my quest to understand the mental, emotional and spiritual factors involved in health and living a life of purpose.

Anthony Hudson

16

Save Others, Save Yourself

*B*eing taken away in an ambulance, falling over a cliff, falling off the roof of a boat, breaking into stranger's house for shelter, slapping my boyfriend, getting sacked, getting into fights with family, friends and strangers, knocking down a large glass ornamental tree are only a few of the stupid, ridiculous, crazy things I did over the years were never a sign to me that I needed to quit drinking. Even when I was locked up in jail overnight, was not enough for me to stop and take notice of what I was doing.

I was killing myself and I didn't or refused to recognise the signs that were so obvious to everyone else. I was brought up in a pub and because drink was everywhere for me, my love for it flew under the radar. I was casually drinking Bacardi and Coke from 14 years of age and drinking heavily since I was 16.

I was on a self-destructive course for years and years and no matter how many times I tried to give up drink, I couldn't. It always had such a powerful hold over me.

I really believe it was a gift from God that faithful day I was jogging up the beach in Lanzarote and saw a girl doing some exercises with these funny looking green rings that got my curiosity to stop her and ask her what they were.

It turns out they are health and wellness tools that were invented by an Austrian tennis player who has Parkinsons Disease. My friend who has Parkinsons lived only a short distance from where we were, so I asked her to come and show the rings to my friend, Breda.

These rings, called smovey, are based on vibration therapy. They are 2 handheld rings with 4 steel balls inside them that when you swing them, the balls create a vibration that activates the reflex zones in the palm of your hand and through he receptors, sends the vibrations up your arms, into your spine, and continues to your brain. My friend had an immediate connection with these rings.

I set up a business in Lanzarote doing classes never realising that these were the tools that were not only going to help my friend but were the tools that would save my life.

Through the continuous action of me using smovey for 15 minutes every day, it was it able to take the urge to drink from me. It also helped with my anxiety and gave me so much clarity that I was able to give up drink.

I only realised a couple of months later that it was the vibrations going through my body activating my vagus nerve and working together with the charkas was the reason I was able to quit so easily.

The vibrations were connecting to my brain and breaking down the addictive chemical and removing the negative energy from my body and replacing it with positive energy.

It was because I wanted to help a friend that I ended up saving my own life and I have never been happier.

It's only now, at 45 years of age, that I am finally sober for 30 months can really appreciate how lucky I am to be alive and in good health.

Irene Treacy

17

You Are Not Done Yet

'*A*m I done? Is this the end of the road for me?' The questions crept through my mind.

When I first started my health business, it flowed effortlessly. But after embracing technology and online marketing, there was no steady predictable flow of clients. Nothing seemed to work. I felt stressed. Overwhelming self-doubt and frustration washed over me. I bottled up negative emotions that pushed me to work harder. To top it all, cigarette smoke from our next-door neighbour triggered endless coughs, dizziness, and a sore throat. My distressed, suffocated lungs gasped for fresh air. I was angry. The body corporate did nothing to protect non-smokers.

I felt trapped. There was no way out but to go within. I worked on healing my anger and resentment towards the situation. I meditated and applied mind tools to balance my perception, which helped restore my inner peace. It was time to move.

While talking to a friend one afternoon, I saw glitzy shapes dancing across the wall. Then my vision blurred. As I stood up, I wobbled like a plate of jelly and couldn't find my balance. That evening, I walked around with an unstable gait. My legs were swinging like a puppet on a string. I laughed at myself while my husband, Tony, watched over me in case I fell.

I told him that my body was undergoing a neurological adjustment and assured him I was fine. The next morning, we went to the beach. I walked barefoot, digging my feet in the sand to massage the acupressure points. I trudged forward then back, alternating every five minutes in an exercise I use to ground my electrical charges. I felt good. I was steady, balanced and normal and the swinging gait was gone.

I felt a familiar sense of healing from within. Nature has always played a big part in my healing. The words 'Rest if you must. You are not done yet', whispered in my mind. The ocean called. I heard and swam back and forth, stretching the meridian pathways, relieving the aches and pains. Like a trusting child, I floated on my back being caressed by the sea. I knew the intelligent body cells would know how to heal themselves. It's nature's way.

After two weeks of observing how I became tired easily, Tony insisted I have medical tests done. Adam, my GP and holistic health practitioner, knew me well. He asked why I was there. "Tony thought I had a stroke," I replied. Adam checked my blood pressure. It was 190/100. He eyed me in such a way that I knew I had to be quiet and let him do his job.

He turned to Tony and outlined stroke neurological symptoms, then handed me a sample strip of blood pressure medication to take. My mind immediately sifted through food sources I could add to our meals that would lower blood pressure. Adam ordered an MRI, cardio, blood tests, and a carotid ultrasound, which showed moderate plaque. The MRI confirmed that I had had a stroke. It puzzled Adam why the other tests were normal. He told me to continue what I was doing and to add methyl folate and B12.

Two months after the stroke, we moved to a beautiful home close to a pristine beach. Today, I no longer push myself against the current. I let go of control and trust the universe. My brain is clearer and can focus on plan-directed action. I feel energetic. My body and mind have continued to heal which has enabled me to work on my mission. The universe guides me through my journey in life. I'm grateful for the past event that contributed to who I am becoming today.

Estelita de Cruz Pearce

18

Choice

J woke with blurred vision, in a foreign environment. I was in a bed that wasn't mine. It was small and firm. A weight pressed through my chest and sunk into my stomach as I realised I was connected to numerous tubes and cords. The sensation engulfed me: 'I'm in hospital! I'm badly hurt!'

I was right. I had been in a single-car accident. Losing control due to an oil slick on a slippery wet highway, I'd wrapped my car around a power pole. The impact was on the driver's side door, which had caused the steering wheel to be pushed close to the middle of the car. In an old car without airbags, I was lucky to be alive.

My injuries were catastrophic. I sustained a severe head injury. This included loss of consciousness, haemorrhagic brain contusions, a cerebrospinal fluid leak through my nose and third nerve palsy which prevented movement of my right eye and eyelid. To add to this, I had facial lacerations and multiple, extensive facial fractures to the front of my skull, mid-face, nose, cheeks, jaw, and right eye orbit. I also sustained lung contusions.

Consequently, I underwent invasive and painful surgeries, including neurosurgery and a facial reconstruction with the insertion of numerous metal pins and plates as well as implants. From hospital, I was admitted into a rehabilitation facility. I felt disorientated from what I can only describe as an immense brain-ache. I was weak, thin, and anemic. My body was not functioning efficiently. The mirrors in hospital had been covered up to avoid the additional distress my reflection might cause. But the mirror in my room at the facility was uncovered, so I diverted my eyes whenever I walked past it.

One day, when I finally felt less groggy, I was alone in my room and it hit me: 'This has really happened!' I wasn't aware how much of an impact what I did next would have. I slowly yet purposely walked to the mirror and raised my eyes to face the truth. The physical result of all the pain and trauma was mirrored back to me. My right eyelid was closed, and I couldn't open it or move my eye. The right side of my face, including my eye socket and cheek, was sunken and my nose was misshaped. I took a deep breath and removed the scarf that covered my half-shaved head to reveal the scar running ear to ear across the top of my head.

I looked hard and cried at my reflection. I raised my chin as I faced the truth and decided, 'I am not a victim! I am alive, and I refuse to give up on myself and my future.' My decision was far more powerful than the result of my accident. I challenged the apparent limitations of my injuries with relentless perseverance to discover ways to heal and create the life I desired. I chose to dedicate myself to looking for the lessons and opportunities in my trauma and turned what could have defeated me into the tragedy that empowered me.

My body began to heal and function properly. I shocked the medical teams with my physical strength and cognitive function. Gradually, I gained control of my eyelid and movement returned in my eye. I can now proudly state that I beat almost every medical odd against me. I am independent, have completed multiple qualifications, established a successful career and travelled internationally. I am blessed to be a mother to two beautiful girls and a wife to my soulmate. I have this life because, in my darkest moment I faced the result of my accident and the pain of my injuries, and I made a choice.

That's when the healing began.

Deborah Stathis

19

An Extremely
Extraordinary Woman

I was 57 years old and at a public speaking course with a fellow attendee, Dr. Mario Alam, who shared his vision, wisdom and story. My soul started to sing; it resonated so deeply I knew my life would never be the same. I was suddenly gifted with the understanding of spirituality, the missing link in my life.

Since my twenties, my life had been one of depression, the darkness becoming denser and deeper with each year. I was drinking daily, binge eating, hiding, on medications, isolated and with constant episodes of hospitalisation. It made no sense. I had survived a childhood that I had not been expected to. I had become a world champion athlete, with a successful business, two kids, and the white picket fence. What the hell is wrong with me? I beat myself up mercilessly, 'How dare I not be healthy and happy!'

Numbness, guilt, and sadness ruled my life. Suicidal thoughts were my constant companion. The scenarios of how to find peace outside my body played repeatedly in my mind. I had made a commitment to my psychiatrist and to my children, 'I will not leave, I will live my life for others.' Entering the voodoo world of spirituality, I was shocked by the freedom, expression, and deep connections that can exist in this world. The spark had been lit.

Numbness disappeared, and instead I was triggered by everything! I hate it, love it! I want more! At first, guilt, shame and embarrassment ruled. I felt hollow, broken and guilty. With support, I went off the meds that weren't working. The withdrawals were horrendous. I stopped drinking and began to see a future, to learn a new language and find a new way. **A-ha** moments came thick and fast. I was confronted, challenged, and invited to see possibilities I had never dreamed of. I was scared and frightened but I wasn't leaving.

I began an affair, opening my heart and learning to receive love. I stopped hiding under baggie clothes. I lost 40 kilos, and went from being unable to look in the mirror, to performing on stage naked, with my daughter and my 80+ year-old parents in the front row.

Unbelievably, I found peace in my body in this lifetime. It was a moment that I had to choose myself or be lost forever. Convulsing, energy rocking through my body, I took my first ever conscious belly breath as an adult and I chose to live my life for myself.

I no longer have a mental health diagnosis. Living my life for others not speaking my truth in order to protect them had kept me alive long enough for me to find my place in a world where I never felt I belonged. I am grateful for every dark moment, the hardships, challenges, bullying, and disconnect that brought me to this incredible moment. The ripple effect of being honest with myself is beautiful.

My business suffered, my ego and pride died multiple times. I constantly and passionately explore what it means to be human, a woman, to live my life for me, to speak my truth and I love it. To find *joy* again is exquisite. Courage, vulnerability, naivety, passion, and love have helped me come home to me and to speak of my journey.

I'm now 58, an empowered woman and storyteller. I'm older, sexy, intelligent, and quirky. Life has never been this good, as I continue to enjoy the affair with the extremely extraordinary woman, me! If you resonate with the dark times, please know you are not alone, and it *always* gets better.

Heather Joy Bassett

20

My Body Spoke Up

At 20 years old, I was living the high life. I ate in gourmet restaurants, throwing back bourbon and cokes like they were Gatorades. I was an athlete in a marathon race, partying hard with friends. At the casino I spent too much, sometimes winning and most times losing, but I enjoyed myself. Having a good time became my drug of choice. Like all addicts, I 'knew' I could stop anytime I wanted. I became tired, constipated, bloated, and was in pain. A mutiny started in my gut. But hey! There was nothing I couldn't handle. After all, I was young. A couple of painkillers would sort out that traitorous body part.

One night, while lying in bed, my stomach began its revolt in earnest. A burning pain like I had never experienced before had me doubled over. The medication I swallowed was just a waste of time. Knees to my chest, I spent a sleepless night in the fetal position. In the morning, I was brutally reminded of the damage I was doing to my body. Stretch marks lined my tummy; my food consumption had increased so much that my skin tore in an effort to cover the new fat my body was racing to store.

My education about food was standard for a normal, healthy Aussie lad. It wasn't rocket science. The food pyramid? What's that? Is that in Egypt? I found myself getting fatter, sicker and sadder. I needed to make a decision about my health and my life!

I knew I didn't want to go the medical route or buy into the pharmaceutical system. I contacted my holistic healer friend. She referred me to a functional doctor for a full blood and body workup. The news was not good. The results were: fatty liver disease, a vitamin D deficiency, low testosterone, and high blood pressure (178/105). Yikes!

As a young man, I had the body of an old stressed geezer. My holistic healing coach devised a meal plan and regime of meditation, mindfulness and meridian exercise. She also taught me how to cook and what nutritional food would support my body's needs. This way, I made a great start to undoing the damage of my previous lifestyle. It was also pleasant having someone keep me accountable.

I'm grateful my body got sick with the way I was living, because now I have turned my whole life around. I've learnt new skills and how to feel good within myself. I have gone from eating absolute garbage to cooking meals that are superb. Now I understand Hippocrates, 'Let food be thy medicine and medicine be thy food.'

I enjoy eating clean foods. I eat organic vegetables, eggs and, meats. I prepare my meals and eat with mindful enjoyment. I try to meditate every day. I have found that my emotional state is far more stable. I have improved in my physical, mental, and gut health. I still occasionally make poor food and drink choices, but I have found that I feel happier and more in control when I eat properly.

I have noticed interesting changes to my hair. It's thicker. My skin is clearer, and my life is happier. I'm consistently shedding excess weight. I don't have as many aches and pains. The longer I maintain this clean way of eating and drinking, the more I improve my overall health. I'm passionate about wellness. I have changed my whole life simply by changing my eating and lifestyle daily habits.

By telling my story, I hope that others will seek out an alternative route to health and wellbeing. Perhaps you can change your life too.

Joshua McNesss

21

Public Face, Private Face

*S*ince early childhood I knew my inner identity, but it wasn't safe to reveal. I internalised many judgements of harsh things expressed in words and actions to and about people like me. I was afraid of being found out and the likely repercussions. Much emotional energy was used in hiding who I was. As my life unfolded, the repression and fear contributed to depression, anxiety, loneliness and declining physical health from the perpetual stress and dis-ease. You see, I am transgender.

I trained in Transpersonal Art Therapy, which included the 'Public Face, Private Face' process. The 'Public Face' aspect of my artwork symbolises how people see me. It is vibrantly colourful and also features a free-spirited bird. The 'Private Face' of the design symbolises my secret self. It is both dark and light. The dark half shows troubled aspects: trauma, brokenness, and intense struggles with mental, emotional, and physical illnesses, and the resulting inner fragmentation of my psyche.

The light half of my 'Private Face' artwork shows beautiful, colourful symbols that represent the treasured core aspect of my identity that I love yet has been kept secret. While people see my outer physical being as male, I know and value the girl and woman I am, though I rarely talked about her, let alone lived as her.

I lived for many decades with intense inner darkness and pain from the repression and oppression until my counselling classmate Dianne witnessed me reveal my full story and the artwork's meaning. With an open mind and heart, she listened with compassion, delight and loving acceptance. The pain and darkness lifted like no other therapy or pill had ever achieved. My spirit soared and I felt free. The next day I felt the same and that has continued each day, increasingly so, for years. Amazing!

The process gave me a way to unlock and express what was trapped within. Loving listening released me, released her. I shared my story and my identity with classmates and was accepted and loved. Thick walls of loneliness and isolation inside me crumbled. I felt like I now belonged.

My spirit dances and soars every time I find new safe, welcoming people and groups, which now includes those in my home. Each time, additional layers of fear and darkness melt away. I am travelling an unfolding journey of liberation and freedom, experimenting and awakening at my own pace. It still is very challenging when I face prejudice and oppression in attitudes and actions, though I am increasingly finding more safe people and places in our society where I am openly known, understood, loved and valued for who I am.

The art therapy process gave me a way to express and share far more than I had previously been able to. It opened the door to revealing what I struggled to make sense of. The deep openhearted listening shows that I am not defective and unlovable. This healing art process was the most significant turning point in my life. A new birthday! Every time I share with safe people, more layers of stress and loneliness dissolve. The love and acceptance of others challenges old painful beliefs and I'm finding deeply healing self-love.

As Emme, I have dramatically experienced the profound healing nature of creativity, openhearted listening, love, acceptance, and belonging. They are everyone's birthright and are free! When we remember who we are, while finding and creating safe places for ourselves and others, we are truly free.

'She remembered who she was, and she was free!'

Emme Krystelle

22

It's a Miracle!

*T*homas was my third child delivered by emergency caesarean three weeks premature. He soon had trouble with his immunity, particularly with episodes of croup and asthma, which hospitalised him six times before he turned three. Finally, I thought he had grown out of croup, as he hadn't had any infections or episodes for about six months.

Then the weather changed, sunny days and icy cold nights. With the cold nights came the dreaded cough again. Dreaded, because we had a previous episode where it developed so quickly he stopped breathing on the way to hospital. I called out 'Help!' to God and got ready to start CPR when he took another ragged breath!

This time I knew the signs; I'd heard this terrible rasping breath on a number of occasions. I threw some essentials into a bag and drove to the hospital. He was admitted immediately. The only sensible thing to do was to climb into the oxygen tent with him, play ball, and read books to provide a distraction and keep him calm and peaceful. There was little the medical staff could do for us because, as they pointed out, it was a virus. They simply said we would have to wait to see if his body could fight it. Not words to greatly encourage this distraught mother!

On the second day, the paediatrician came and left without saying very much. Thomas' fever and croup had sapped his strength. On the third day he struggled to breathe. The paediatrician came with a solemn face saying, "There's nothing else we can do. I'm sorry but I don't think he's going to make it through the night." Those words echoed in my brain! Then a supernatural peace washed over me, and a fighting spirit stirred inside. "No," I said. "I know there's something else you can do, maybe an old remedy, but there's something else you can do." He shook his head and walked away.

I grabbed the phone and told my husband. I rang relatives and friends in churches all up the East Coast of Australia, so people could pray with us. The paediatrician walked back in later that night and said, "We'll try a series of injections, I don't have any faith in them, but we'll try." I said I would stay while they gave the injections. They said it would be very dangerous and painful so I should leave. I said, "No." I stayed with him helping to hold him and reassure him in case he pulled away or became upset. I prayed to God that he would not pull or twist himself and hurt himself during the injections. Amazingly, he was exhausted. He slept and just groaned and rolled over. His ragged breathing went on. "I'm sorry," said the paediatrician.

"The only other thing we can do is insert a tube in his trachea. But it isn't likely to work because of the amount of swelling in the voice box." I turned to the paediatrician and said, "I know he's going to be fine. We have many people praying." The paediatrician shook his head and walked away. I prayed to God to give him strength.

The minutes ticked by, then the hours. The sun peeped over the horizon. He was still breathing! When the paediatrician returned, he scratched his head! "It's a miracle!" he said. Two days later, we went home, a lot quicker than the staff expected and he never had croup again. I'm so glad God answered our prayers. We are so proud of Thomas, who is now a strong man that works supporting those who have disabilities.

Delwyn Webb

23

Healing in the Fast Lane

"Can not eating for 32 days save my life?" His voice on the phone was my last hope of finding someone that knew what to do with my body, which was shutting down. I was holding back tears of fear and disbelief as I heard him say, "You need to stop taking all medications right now. Stop eating, drink only juice for at least 21 days, and then take only water for at least ten days."

This seemed insanely dangerous and did not make any sense to me. How can I survive on this, especially on only water? There was silence on the phone as I tried to surrender into this and trust him. My heart and body were saying 'yes', but my mind was in control and took over.

I will starve to death! That was what I was thinking! Then I heard the words I needed to hear. Straightforward words that made me take full responsibility of my health for the very first time in my life.

"Tami, take these labels off yourself. These are bullshit labels created to give 'symptoms' of a body in 'disease' a name, and then a medication for you to treat the labeled symptom like it is some disease in its own entity."

Silence filled the air. I couldn't believe he was even talking to me like this. He was rude, obnoxious and arrogant. I felt insulted and sick in the gut from anxiety. I was close to hanging up on him, but didn't.

Tyler continued, "Have the medications helped you heal? Have any of the neurologists or GPs helped you heal? Are you any better than you were a year ago?" His confidence intimidated me but I kept listening. I answered "No" and felt my heart sink.

I'd been going around in circles, still having days I couldn't hold my two-year-old girl on my lap because my fatigue and pain were so severe. Some days my husband had to help me to the toilet, so I wouldn't fall. Why was I placing trust in drugs and people for so long when they had not helped me? The words 'doctor knows best' lingered in my mind. "If we focus on healing your gut for a month, you will heal. It's all in your gut," he said with so much belief. With a stern passion and urgency, he asked me, "When are you going to take back control of your health? When?" I took a breath and stepped into the fast lane of healing.

"Now," I answered. Instantly, a light ignited in my body. This was it! I knew it. I immediately stopped taking medications and started the journey. I flew to Bali to be close to Tyler as I did my fast. I fasted on juices for 25 days and water for seven days. It was the most intensely beautiful journey back to myself and I healed!

Since then I've completed many five, ten, and 14-day water fasts, and five 21-day juice fasts. Physically, emotionally and spiritually, I changed and grew into a happy, healthy and active mother of two, now doing for others what Tyler did for me: teaching them to heal in the fast lane. I'm forever grateful for Tyler's messages.

Tami Jane

24

A Journey of Self-Empowerment

*F*or sale! One 42-year-old obese, alcoholic, depressed, and suicidal female. Would you buy this?

I was adopted at birth and was always looking to find belonging with others. My two younger brothers were not adopted. My father would go to my brothers' soccer and cricket games but would never go to anything of mine, even when I made it to the Opera House for Physical Culture. I always felt like I was not not good enough. Someone who did not want me had given me away at birth. I was unlovable. I was always trying to please people because I felt this would make them like me. I would change my personality to match theirs and to try to fit in.

I did not even know who the real me was. I knew deep down that I was always meant to help people. The search for acceptance began early. I changed careers and worked in the training space, starting with Optus Communication in their learning and development department. I loved the job but, unfortunately, I kept getting sick.

I had become epileptic at the age of 27. I blamed the epilepsy for ruining this new form of acceptance I had discovered. I had a seizure, two days before my menstrual period was due. I was heavily medicated. My CT scans and MRIs were always normal and the doctors could not explain it. While I was lucky to be working for Optus, who accepted me for my 'illness', other companies would not have been as understanding.

In addition to the epilepsy, I was 130 kg, which was not helping my health. I tried everything to lose the weight, but nothing would work. In 2010, I opted to have a weight reduction operation, and thought that once I had become skinny, all of the problems I was facing would go away. How wrong I had been! My problems were exacerbated, making me feel like I was the victim and the world owed me something. Again, these feelings stemmed from my adoption, even though my adoptive parents have loved and nurtured me the best way they could. This negative perception of myself and the epilepsy continued for many years.

In 2015, I decided that living this life was no longer for me. The five anticonvulsants and two antidepressants I was taking every morning were sending me into a downward spiral and making matters worse. I was on my way to an appointment with the neurologist, sitting in a food court with my mother, when the neurologist walked in and sat next to us. I smiled and said "Hello." By the look on his face, he obviously did not recognise me. My mother had a look of horror on her face and said, "He does not know who you are." Even though I had been seeing him, sometimes three times a month, he still did not know who I was.

Through an amazing naturopath, I stopped taking all medication, and have never looked back! I also commenced my path of personal development and started to utilise hypnotherapy and NLP to help me remove the underlying feelings that were causing me all this pain. Hypnotherapy saved my life. It helped me overcome my crippling depression. No longer do I spend days in bed feeling like the world is against me.

Now I am a hypnotherapist, working with people to overcome anxiety and depression, completely quit smoking, and lose excess kilos. My life is now so full of hope and joy. Each day is fulfilling, knowing I am helping others achieve the happiness that life offers, just like I have found.

Alison Morris

25

Life After Miscarriage

*I*t was 1996: I was working in financial marketing in London. In my work, I was motivated and driven. I was someone who got things done. I was flexible and liked to make things happen for people. I was organised and hard working. My family was in New Zealand, so my friends were my main support.

My boyfriend and I had been together for a couple of years when I unexpectedly fell pregnant. We were both in shock. We had a long chat about our future and decided to get married. After our 12-week scan, we announced it to our friends, family and colleagues at work. Whilst it was a surprise, we were thrilled about becoming parents. I felt changes in my body and morning sickness had kicked in. I was excited and nervous – life was about to change.

At the time of our 20-week scan, I was feeling eager to hear the tiny little heartbeat and see how much the little fingers and toes had grown. I lay down on the table, staring intently at the screen. I knew instantly that something was wrong. There was an interminable silence from the stenographer, who got up and left the room to get a second opinion. She didn't tell me what was wrong.

I waited to see the consultant, as there was something that didn't look right. In that moment, time slowed down, I felt sick with a sense of dread and panic, yet total calm denial that anything could go wrong. Eventually, the consultant took me into her office and explained that there was amniotic fluid inside the baby and not enough in the sac. The news wasn't great. We had to make a decision to terminate or let things transpire naturally. We were told to go home over the weekend and decide.

I felt lost, numb, and empty. We returned on Monday to be told that our baby boy had died. I was inconsolable; this little being I had carried for 23 weeks was no longer. I felt dead inside and wanted to be alone.

My journey since then has taken me on a path of self-discovery and healing. I was looking for a way to change my life and discovered my vocation was complementary therapies and energy healing. I met incredible teachers who helped me to release my hurt and trauma. I found comfort from the Buddhist teachings around loss and how souls sometimes come back for a short time to finish their work.

I felt many emotions; from pain, depression and guilt, to feeling lonely, isolated and overwhelmed. I felt hurt and jealous when I saw a baby or someone who was pregnant. I felt sad when my partner did his best but didn't know how I needed comforting.

In time, I was able to heal and feel ready to start a family again. I now have two daughters and, although I'll never forget my first baby, I have found love, peace, and joy once more. Losing my baby has led me to what I am supposed to be doing. It was one almighty wake-up call, but one I'm now grateful for. Studies have shown those who find meaning from trauma heal quicker.

What lights me up now is enabling women to get to a place of happiness and joy in life. My mission is to help women get through their pregnancy loss, so they can look back one day and say, 'It was something that has enabled me to move forward. Something that I now find meaning from, something that was the hardest thing in my life but has shaped me for the better.'

Jo Tocher

26

The Wonders of My Mindset

I have been a video gamer most of my life, paying no attention to the outside world. After leaving school at 17, I began working at a retail company. Two years later, while working at the checkouts, two men approached my register. One of them stood in front of me holding 2 large bags of DVD's, and the other behind me holding a knife to my throat and telling me to let his friend go past. I had no choice but to do as he said while mentally taking notes to give to the police.

I was fearful it would happen again, and as a result, developed acute stress disorder escalating into depression. I began taking medication. Unable to work, I used gaming as a form of escape, drinking 30-40 litres of Coke a week and scoffing takeaways. This went on for a year until my brother said to me there is more to life than a computer screen, and that I should enjoy life and head back to work to earn real gold, rather than gold in a game.

It made me think that I could die this way with nothing to show for my life. So that was it, I decided that it was time to change. My father had just been diagnosed with diabetes, which made me think about my own body. I looked around my computer and all the Coke bottles. A visit to the doctor and tests showed my blood sugar, cholesterol, and vitamin levels were all fine, but my blood pressure was 162/132. The doctor warned me that if I continued down the same path, heart problems, diabetes, or death could be my end.

So, I picked myself up, threw out the soft drinks, and drank only water. I gradually adapted to eating healthily and began exercising, which is one of the best treatments for depression. I took training courses and learnt new skills to be able to get into a new job and focus on living my life again. Getting off the couch and focusing on living a life where I check things off my bucket list has been amazing. I have 20,000 things on that list I would like to achieve, of which I have completed some 3,000 of them in the last six years or thereabout.

From all the money I saved by not spending on unhealthy food, I have been able to have incredible adventures. In the last few years I have ridden a helicopter and landed at the peak of both glaciers in Southern New Zealand; I became an author and wrote a book, *My Never-Ending Journey of Life;* I ran an all-night ultra-marathon of 55 kilometres in 12 hours; I abseiled face-forward down an eight-story building, traversed caverns, and pushed my body through caves the size of a steering wheel.

There have been a lot of personal challenges and roadblocks I have faced while pushing my body to live healthier. You can go from feeling strong and amazing to feeling upset and struggling all in one day as you take your body past its comfort zone to places way beyond its reach. The key is to be kind to yourself on the journey. Some days are better than others.

My weight loss from giving up soft drinks was dramatic: from 200 kg down to 140 kg. I have not only lost kilograms, but so much emotional baggage as well. While all the feelings I suffered when I was overweight didn't vanish overnight, I learned a lot about self-worth through diet, exercise and perserverance.

Lance Garbutt

27

Stepping into Marcia

*B*eing the youngest of four children with a 13-year gap, I grew up feeling like the only child with 'five' parents telling me what to do and guiding me. I was overprotected and spoiled because everything was done for me. Having experienced heavier periods over the years, I discovered in 2007 that I had huge uterine fibroids, leading to heavy menstrual bleeding.

I had tried all the different alternative approaches and I knew that eventually the only solution would be a full hysterectomy; the size and location of the fibroids indicated that removing the fibroids wouldn't be an option.

The most powerful and painful moment I remember is being alone in a small hotel room in Sydney on September 30th, 2009, while attending a three-day conference. In the middle of that day, I went to the toilet and had this huge blood loss. I panicked! It really hit me hard that I could literally die that day.

I knew for the next few hours that it was all up to me. I remembered saying to someone prior that, "I would rather bleed to death than have a hysterectomy." As the words came out of my mouth, I realised how inflexible I was and that keeping this belief was literally killing me. Now, alone in my room, I was faced with a question: 'Do I have a WHY to live?'

The decision was mine and no one else could do anything for me. During those 18 dark hours I was on a tightrope between life and death. I decided to step out of that little girl who always had someone to protect her and make decisions for her, and I grabbed my own power and took charge of my life. Stranded against my own mental wall with nowhere else to go, I first considered the possibility of undergoing a hysterectomy.

Life has interesting ways of nagging us to grow up, and that shift in mindset saved my life. I managed to find a surgeon who agreed to perform the least invasive procedure possible. As I was waiting for the surgery to happen, I did what was needed to do – I got my haemoglobin levels back to normal and even took some hormones to induce premature menopause and reduce the bleeding. During that waiting period, I could have bled to death at any moment. Undergoing the hysterectomy not only saved my life, it also gave me new levels of physical vitality.

Looking back on that agonising experience, I realised that every time I was bleeding heavily, I was subordinating to others. I was giving my power away and letting my life force slowly drain out of me. Basically, I was ignoring my responsibility and not standing in my own truth. I was taking myself for granted and not acknowledging my own brilliance.

Since that day I have certainty that I am the one responsible for my life, and can create whatever I want. I have been more connected with my inner voice. It has given me the courage to leave a job, step out of the conventional box and step into my own business to follow my purpose. The experience taught me that, 'every experience in life is guiding us to step into our authentic self.'

I dropped the anchor of security and I am now sailing off on my own, living my mission inspiring and empowering others to embrace their brilliance and be the creator of their own lives.

Dr. Marcia Becherel

28

A Love Letter to Myself

*B*eing the first-born and only daughter and granddaughter on my mother's side, I was happy enough growing up. I threw myself into sports, dancing, art, and reading, and had lots of friends. So why didn't I believe in myself? Why did I feel I was never smart enough, interesting enough, tall enough, pretty enough, thin enough?

I was given the message 'I'm not enough.' I focused on being accepted and validated. I loved to be told I was enough. It never was. This mindset kept me stressed, anxious, and stagnant. It contributed to developing illness from emotional, mental, and sexual abuse, leading to multiple surgeries and treatments. I always strived to be perfect, yet all I felt was doubt, guilt, and indecisiveness.

Through it all, I developed an inner resilience that kept me on the path of light. I knew with some degree of certainty that stepping down into the abyss of darkness would lead to more pain, struggle and a long climb to freedom.

After ending a nine-year relationship, I realised that in not loving myself, I made the other person feel uncertain about me and I pushed them away. I thought I was unlovable: the nicer they were to me, the more I acted out on my own insecurities. Consequently, they felt unloved, and then I started feeling unloved. I perpetuated the ending that I had been afraid of from the beginning because of my own fear of love.

My *'aha moment'* was a kaleidoscope of dizzy-inducing, power-zapping moments that led to one big moment of certainty: that I had come to a place where I could fully say I loved myself and that I was enough. In this moment I felt strong, genuine and whole. From then on, I was able to stay true to myself. I gained strength from knowing that, in loving myself, I couldn't blame anyone else; I could take responsibility for my life, and in doing so, I was led to freedom from fear, and light from the dark.

I started saying 'no' instead of 'yes', and people didn't stop liking me. There was some resistance from family members, but I stood my ground and believed I deserved to be respected. The only person I needed validation from was myself. With self-love came more opportunities, more confidence, a stronger voice, and a focused and motivated mind from which I am now more in touch with my needs and desires. I have adopted new ideas to lead me forward. I have taken more chances, and as a result, have come to believe in myself.

Since learning to love myself, relationships are much easier. I realised I am worth being treated with respect and integrity, just as the other person, who I have deemed worthy of the same treatment. If you don't love yourself, then it is a struggle to give both yourself and others what is needed.

I have recently purchased a property that needs complete renovation which I have the confidence to project manage myself. In the past, when I didn't love myself, I couldn't make a phone call to order a pizza let alone ring 20 tradies, organise quotes, and source suppliers. I have been told that I inspire others and I have taken that on board by continuing to plan opening a holistic guesthouse in my local area.

To complete yourself, love and accept who you are. That's what this is all about. You can't be strong all the time. Your mind can't differentiate between what someone else tells you and what you tell yourself. So be kind to yourself. I looked in the mirror, took a deep breath and said, 'I love you, Maria.' And you smiled back at me.

Maria Solano

29

There Is Always a Choice

*J*n 2014, I turned 30 and graduated from a psychology degree. I'd had hopes of becoming a 'super important doctor', make my parents proud, and ultimately find fulfilment in a career where I could help people. This involved four years of endless anxiety, stress and undetected unhappiness – killing myself in pursuit of high grades.

It was in Italy that I woke up one morning with a blurry eye, later confirmed to be optic neuritis. I was referred for an MRI on my return to New Zealand, as this was a symptom of Multiple Sclerosis (MS).

I will always remember lying in that MRI machine – as still as death – with tears pouring down my cheeks and silently questioning, 'what if I am dealt a really bad fate?' Despite the potential possibility, I distinctly remember a calmness wash over me. My heart was full and peaceful as I realised I would die a happy girl – I had many recent successes, the greatest being visiting Poland (my Dad's mother-country) and seeing him skip the streets with glee like a little kid. This had been a bucket-list dream of mine.

As I sat in the neurologist's office, the white dots on my brain scan were familiar to me: lesions. "It's okay, it's okay," I heard myself say out loud to calm my mum. "You don't actually qualify for a diagnosis," the neurologist informed me. "You have lesions, but due to solely one symptomatic episode, only in Australia would you qualify as having MS." Immune-suppressant drugs were offered and turned down; I decided I would take care of myself instead, despite no known cause or cure.

Skip to Melbourne, Australia, a year later. I was working at a job in which I was severely unhappy and 'stuck'. Physical pain mirroring my emotional pain increased for nine months, until one day when I could neither stand up nor walk, and I was forced back in that MRI. An Australian neurologist handed me the diagnosis this time. Again, I refused drugs.

To relieve the emotional (and physical pain), I quit my job, learnt mindfulness, got back into meditation, subsequently threw out the chocolate and wine, and was taken through a process of energetic, emotional and subconscious 'clearing', which changed my life. I spent a year in intensive physiotherapy too, and in four months could dance again.

Caught up in my new life, I returned for my routine MRI after finding the referral buried in emails. This time I received an urgent personal call from my neurologist – she had received the results. "Are you okay Danielle? Do you need to go to emergency?" she asked. "Um, what?" I almost laughed. I was BETTER than okay, I was so well. "Your MRI is EXTREMELY abnormal. You should be very sick!" she replied.

I remember messaging my friend after this and saying, "What if this is what it's all for? What if this is the point? What if I am supposed to do this differently so that I can show others how to do this differently? How incredible would that be? I can't give up on myself and my health – not only for me, but for other people." And that is when I realised that we have a choice. I had a choice; we always have a choice.

And since that day I chose not to have a diagnosis and continue to live symptom-free (with and) without MS, and it feels so good.

Dannii Orawiec

30

Where Is My Mom?

*I*t was a beautiful spring day. After spending the day at the lake to see how far the ice had melted, my buddies and I were swapping stories and laughing while dad drove us home. My 9-year-old self couldn't wait for a summer of swimming and playing at the beach. On the way, a car sped towards us, lights flashing and horn blaring. As both cars stopped, the passenger door burst open and my mom tumbled out screaming, "He's dead! He's dead! Bobby's dead!"

My elder brother was dead. I instinctively pulled my little brother closer to me and watched, not fully comprehending the scene before me: Mom screaming and wailing, pounding her fists on the hood of the car and Dad doing his best to console her. Over the next several days I hovered on the fringe of a mysterious adult world, quietly observing my mom as visitors came and went, each one triggering a renewed bout of anguish. Then came the funeral, and the transformation of my mother.

I waited for my familiar loving mother to return, but she didn't. My 'new' mother sought solace from a bottle, and my dad eventually did the same. Our home became an after-hour party venue. It didn't matter whether it was a school night and children needed sleep. Waiting for our parents to stop drinking and their friends to go home became our bedtime story.

Anger, hatred, and frustration began to fester within me and manifested as a leg twitch and an acute nervous stomach. I fought mental battles and experienced nightmares in which I screamed at my mom, demanding her to see me and to change back into the mother I had once known. Pouring my anger into positive undertakings like sports and school spilled over into reckless behaviour and binge drinking. I did everything I could to make myself visible to my mother. It didn't work, the bottle always won.

My anger continued through my 20s and 30s. Although I refused to acknowledge my mother, I had angry dreams even after her death in 1989: 25 years after Bobby's death. One morning, after yet another wild night of partying, I realised that I was becoming my mother. I had to change. I began meditating to quiet my angry mind. Meditation slowly began to change me. I became calmer, the nightmares lessened, I partied less and I began to pay attention to my thoughts and actions.

Then a miracle happened in 1996. As I meditated, my mother began to speak to me of her pain and suffering, and I began to feel her love. I came to understand that she hadn't meant to hurt me. She hadn't known how to release her pain. Her returning to tell me was a sign of her love; I felt it coursing through me. I understood how I had kept my anger alive with a sense of victimhood, and accepted responsibility for my own healing. Mom's gift gave me the strength to change.

I continued to meditate, deepen my connection to spirit, and listen to the quiet voice within. I also read voraciously, and began to heal myself. The ups and downs of life are handled with ease and an inner wisdom that knows what to do. After years of striving for attention, I'm comfortable with who I am and where I am.

Today, I'm surrounded by love and abundance and I love life. Life has become easier, less stressful and more joyous. Now, when my mom comes to mind, I smile and send her love.

Carolynne Melnyk

31

Beyond Personal Development

*W*hen I decided to write my healing story, I wondered what I really had to say about healing. It's not like I've ever had some severe, life-threatening illness. What I have experienced is a lifelong longing for some level of emotional fulfilment. To have the sense that I am a worthwhile human being and that I have the capacity to enjoy this life, instead of feeling like I am worthless and I have no purpose. That's a good foundation for addiction, although it's one thing I said I'd never do. I was wrong.

Becoming an addict was easy. It started with schoolyard bullying and using video games at a young age to deflect feeling like a social invalid. Add pornography to avoid the anxiety of approaching women. Add personal development, which became its own addiction to building fantasies of greatness to avoid my real challenges. Add overcoming my anxieties around women to falling into a deep infatuation with a heroine junkie, stripper, prostitute.

As a result, drugs entered my life. Then, I had a woman who travelled across the world to give herself to me and when I finally got the message, she took it away, rightly. Hence, grief and loss entered my life for the first real time and this spiralled me down into a pit of self-loathing that lasted seven years.

I became addicted to psychedelics. It stirred me to explore yoga, meditation and inspiring visions, but most importantly, a real, visceral re-connection to my body that helped me feel comfortable in it. It became my tool for creativity, enlightenment, and understanding, which brought me many heart-opening moments. It even helped me overcome my fear of singing in front of others, allowing the musician inside me to come out and play. But over time, and with a new family to provide for, it also brought me a disconnection from love, a physical disorder and the same lack of purpose I was using it to find.

Ending an addiction is harder than it seems. People use an addiction to survive pain and that pain is the belief that you are worthless. What I learnt through my own inner work is that addiction and grief share this common root. See, we can just as easily be addicted to grief as we can be to a more positive feeling, or a behaviour that we compulsively repeat. It's the grief of not appreciating what was given before it was lost and the grief of not giving enough before the opportunity died. Both of these create a deep self-hatred which gets masked externally in a story of loss, giving us the ability to point to someone else leaving our life as the cause of our suffering; it's an attempt to avoid a worse feeling.

That's what I want you to know, because it's that idea of fair appreciation that finally healed me from what I thought I'd never fully restore myself from. I learnt that the education I most needed was the class on appreciating both myself and others, for our mutual and exchanged capacities and powers, creating meaning for each other in the process. Without this, it's impossible to heal, because all wounds are there to remind us of those tenets of value.

I will always remember the day I learnt how to appreciate the woman who flew across the world to me and what we gave to each other. The simplest of truths was born out of the hardest journey; there was no loss, just a loss of loving.

Stephan Gardner

32

From Bullied to Empowered

As I lay face down in the dirt after being knocked to the ground, I thought, 'Why me? Why do I have to go through this daily?' I was defeated and kicked multiple times whilst I lay on my stomach waiting for the final hit. Finally, they ran off with the person who filmed the fight, just before a family member came and picked me up; one of the only people who could potentially help me through the experience of hell they call school. I couldn't tell this same person that I was struggling so we drove home in silence.

The short drive to my house felt like forever, I went to my room and lay there trying not to feel emotions. Over the years, I had become good at bottling them up.

For years, I physically rocked on the way to school, mentally dreading to go. Bullies were there on the bus, the schoolyard, in class. One girl stood up in the classroom and yelled that nobody liked me. Two others in art class also bullied me, and the teacher moved one of them right next to me. In PE class we were running laps and one kid threw sticks at me, one after another after each lap. It got to the point where I decided I needed to defend myself. I had enough, I looked around and picked up a big stick, walked over and hit him across his hip. After years of playing tennis and cricket, I produced a decent swing. Another time at the swimming pool, one kid picked me up and threw me towards the pool, I hit the edge with my back and fell in.

I questioned who I was, and what I was doing at school. Why do I keep coming? What's the point of going to school to live in fear, feel horrible about yourself, and constantly have to watch your back and suppress your emotions hoping to not let the bullies affect you? What kind of life is that?

Losing fights badly, my self-esteem was gone. I had zero confidence, hated myself, and hit rock bottom. Something needed to change. The only person that I knew would be able to do this was myself. I just needed a bit of guidance along the way

My brother-in-law took me to the gym to get bigger and stronger so I could defend myself and beat the crap out of anyone who put their hands on me again – a very reactive and aggressive motivation. I knew this wouldn't be easy, but I wanted it. I got stronger and bigger, it gave me a sense of power, confidence and self-esteem. I started to like myself and my body. My motivation shifted to become more empowering. I wanted to feel confident, strong, and to like the look of my body.

I was once a shy kid who hated himself, who was ashamed of himself physically and mentally insecure with many ups and downs. I was soul searching, finding out my values, empowering beliefs and passion. I have become more loving, self-aware and confident. I am now able to talk to people with confidence and not fear what they think of me. I can speak in front of groups and have started my own mind body transformation business. I can talk to the opposite sex with confidence. I have been able to find my passion to serve others vocationally as well as though volunteer work.

To know your worth is one of the most powerful things that you can have; finding your strengths, your positive traits, and what you love to do. Who you are as a person is defined by what you decide and love about youself, not what other people think of you. It has opened so many more life-changing experiences up for me.

Jason Russell

33

My Pure Transformation to Love

I always believed that I was truly a bad person; beaten from a young age and starting therapy after seeing my mum raped when I was nine. I thought it was my fault that mum didn't love me. Life was hard. But nothing compared to the life we took on after my mum remarried. I suffered physical, emotional and mental abuse, which lead me down a deep path of clinical depression, anxiety and PTSD.

On many occasions, I have been so desperate that I have tried to end my life, each time more painful and waking up with more pain and despair. I turned to alcohol and bulimia to get me through. I felt unworthy and useless. I was never enough, never appreciated, and unlovable. This impacted all of my relationships.

I always wanted to help others; hence, I became a psychiatric nurse, then an army medic. During this time, I was free from depression, bulimia and IBS. I became able to manage the PTSD I had lived with for six years after giving birth to my stillborn baby all alone. But it merely masked the symptoms. I always felt alone, always felt ashamed and fearful, scared and lonely inside.

I met my husband and I stopped taking drugs and looked forward to having our son. That's when, the depression crept in again; I felt unworthy, not good enough, unlovable.

When I studied NLP, coaching, energy medicine, and EFT (emotional freedom techniques), I was able to finally give up the alcohol that I desperately craved all day long. Life became great. 'Then a famiy trauma hit us. It was horrific. We lost our home, our business, and our peace of mind. My husband and I drifted apart, and I blamed myself for everything.

Having suffered post-natal depression with each of my four babies, each time progressively worse than before, I finally ended up in psychiatric care – broken and with psychosis. I couldn't be strong anymore; it was a relief to hit rock bottom. Being back on pills and in therapy was a blessing. After being in hospital for emergency surgery after my sterilisation went horribly wrong, I was able to make it home on Christmas Eve. I was lucky to be alive and I knew things had to change; I had to change. The turn of a new year was such a pivotal time for me.

With my marriage in tatters and full of anger; something had to give. It was me. It was so hard. I had so much pain in my body, my joints ached, my head always hurt, I could barely sleep at night. I hated myself, my life, and the loneliness and anxiety that ate away at me.

The pinnacle moment in my healing journey was learning that I truly did not love myself. It was from this moment of raw transparency that I was able to truly heal myself of the depression, the trauma, all of the PTSD, the anxiety and pain. I started applying every tool, modality and technique that I had into making myself the mum that my children could be proud of, not the one crying in the bathroom every five minutes wishing I could disappear.

My life now is way different from what it used to be. I am now a shining happy person who bounces out of bed, free from physical and emotional pain. I am excited to be alive, to have my children, my amazing husband, my best friend, and a support network of women who I have met on my healing journey to becoming a true vibrational match to the love and life that I always dreamed of. I am now changing the lives of other women who were living with trauma and helping them to be free.

Life is amazing, and so am I.

Jeani Howard

34

On The Rough Road To Redemption

*M*y earliest memory goes back to when I was six years old. I found my mum unconscious in the bathroom, lying in her vomit and I remember that I was unable to wake her. This was one of many that I recall. The negativity and depression in our household was sometimes unbearable. My parents were not ideally suited for each other and it came to a point where dad was done. After a few suicide attempts, he eventually succeeded when he shot himself on the 15th of July 1996.

People in the village said things to me like, "You must really hate your father now." It never even crossed my mind to hate him. Nor my mother, even though I felt that she should have done things differently, at the time. I understood more about the whole situation much later in life. In 1999 I moved to New Zealand. I believe that was the time when my healing journey began. After the novelty of being in another country had worn off, I started to experience depression. I also gained a lot of weight.

The pain in my body also became a problem and soon the pain medication was not really working anymore. Having a real repulsion to medication, because of growing up in a household where mum was dependent on it, I refused to even think about taking an antidepressant. So, I started acupuncture. After my tenth session, Karen, my Acupuncturist said that she felt that it was time to now work on my emotions. She gave me the name of a Certified BodyTalk Practitioner (CBP) in Auckland and four days later I had my first session.

I still remember receiving my first session like it was yesterday; everything made so much sense. It was fascinating, and I was intrigued. Within 20 minutes, I knew that I was going to study this modality. After my session, I drove back home over the Harbour Bridge. It was winter and raining – it was quite a bleak day – but suddenly, it struck me: it felt like somebody had lifted the curtain and I was able to see the colours of life again. I started crying, I felt like I had come home and deep healing had just occurred.

Over the next few months, I had more sessions and I felt better and better. I felt lighter, and there was a joy I could feel deep within me, as well as hope. I used to play scenarios over and over in my head, but after my sessions I realised that, while I had the memory, there were no emotional attachments left. It was fascinating!

The pain in my body also started to subside, and I got better sleep too. I felt like I wanted to be fully present within my life and this modality was able to provide that for me. I have never looked back. In 2008, I started my very first module with the BodyTalk System. Today, I have the privilege to work with people in my own clinic, and I cannot think of anything else I would like to do.

In 2012, my mum was tired and also decided to take her own life. I don't think I could have coped without the teachings and philosophies of BodyTalk, and how it helped me process and heal emotions and active memory. Mum and dad were souls who had a heavy burden to carry and no tools to work with. They did the best they could, they taught me a lot, and it is because of them that I now have an understanding of people who need compassion and healing.

Andrea Baumann

35

Growing My Soulmate

*W*ant to read a feel-good story? Where boy meets girl, they fall in love and live happily ever after. Sorry. Let me tell you what really happened. Many years ago, I found – or so I thought – the lady of my dreams. We were going to get married, have a family, build a fantastic career, and so on. It didn't happen quite like that.

The marriage lasted six years, and our child was born after we separated. She was married to 'the other man' within a month of divorcing. My 'perfect life' had crumbled, leading to several sad years of loneliness, frustration and even anger. I had no faith in relationships. I was living proof that the 'perfect relationship' does not exist.

Meanwhile, there was a lady called Maree with her own set of problems, including a bunch of unpleasant incidents between her and her husband, and a failed marriage. So, here were two 'lost souls', both feeling that relationships do not work, though for different reasons. Dilemma! Is this what life was really like? Is this all there was? How come there were so many 'apparently' happy and successful marriages in the world.

Maree and I met and became good friends. We had many discussions about 'the opposite sex'. Of course, as we grew closer, we experienced the same things all couples, even friends, experience: differences of opinions, frustration with each other, and so on. But no romance! In the background, and as part of my work, I was researching how human beings, like nature itself, have a natural way of doing things, and that if communicated effectively, our natural gifts, our talents, could be of value to others. I was fascinated by this and drew Maree into my world.

We both loved learning about our true selves and how people could really engage, if only they knew 'the secret' was being yourself and letting others be themselves. This simple fact changed our relationship. We were beginning to really understand and appreciate each other as a couple. The little niggles that most couples experience were still there, but there was awareness and a commitment to listen, accept, and engage.

Our relationship blossomed. We spent all our time together, our romantic life grew, and all seemed rosy. Like all couples, there were disagreements, but we now knew how to get past those and connect effectively. She knew me. I knew her. We were always on the same page, even if from different perspectives. Is this what a 'soulmate' was?

We had learnt a valuable lesson in life: the 'physical' does not last, the 'romantic nights' slow down. We realised that physical 'love' is transient. Many younger people base their potential success with their partner mostly on looks and a willingness to 'be close' physically. And they wonder why they have problems when age gets in the way. We believe that real soulmates look past the 'façade' and see the person. They engage with the other person's natural talents and see ongoing synergy through understanding. They 'click' on so many more levels than just the physical.

Being with Maree, my soulmate, has changed my life. We spend all our time together, both at home and work. We love our life together and each other. Maree and I have discovered, firsthand, those destined for long-lasting relationships with the 'right person' seek to grow their soulmate, not wait for them to magically appear.

Growing your soulmate is priceless.

Jeff Withers

36

When Life Fails You

J had it all – well, I thought I did – a six-figure career, a steady relationship, lovely home, health, family, and friends. It was 2013 when I decided to take more responsibility for myself. I made big changes around my health and wellbeing, left my corporate career and became a personal trainer. It took me so long, but I had finally felt what true happiness was: a deep connection to self, life, nature and the world. I loved sharing my knowledge, empowering my clients, watching them overcome their boundaries and achieve success. But, on the inside, I was empty.

My mind only knew how to be a 'perfectionist'. I didn't know how to run a business; I didn't know how to ask for help without feeling like a fraud or a failure. I felt so alone. Every day, I went deeper and deeper into a hole. It was hard to be chirpy for my 5 a.m. clients when I barely had the strength to get out of bed. Some days, I cancelled sessions on clients. I stopped caring about everything, even eating. I couldn't find the sunshine in my days anymore. I wanted to save everyone else from the pain I believed they were feeling from my failures.

The day I planned to ease all the pain, I texted my sister. She somehow knew what I meant. I was ready to check out of life. She called straight away, and during our talk I realised how selfish and inwardly-focused I had become. I hadn't considered the pain she, my partner, and my nephews would feel if I continued with my suicide plan. When I told my partner the pain I had been feeling, the emotional chains broke with his words, "You have not failed." For so long, I believed that if I failed, I would lose the love from those who mattered to me. These conversations were telling me otherwise.

The realisation that there was nothing to 'fail' at, and that I actually had achieved through the act of trying, meant there was some small hope that I could experience happiness again. I created the problem so I could 'uncreate' the problem. Deep within, I knew life could be different. For things to change, my only option was small steps and belief in myself. And it had to start now.

I turned my focus to my inner wisdom, and the answers started flowing. I wrote a list of things I could do to lift my focus and energy, and committed to doing them each day. Then I crafted a money affirmation to say before sleep. I made my partner say it with me as I didn't have the strength to say it alone or believe it to be true initially. Finally, I asked my books which one of them would serve me best, and *The Law of Attraction* presented itself. I knew this was the book that would help me find myself again.

That night, I opened the book to the tattered receipt that had been used as a bookmark five years earlier. I cried when I opened it. Each night from then, it slowly unlocked the filing cabinets in the dark room of my mind. It showed me that I did know how to handle life, that I could achieve a level of peace and self-love, and see life as a blessing again, despite the journey I had been on.

I started reconnecting with friends, relearning about food, and being fully present. Colour came back into my soul lifting the darkness and the heaviness. It was a sense of relief that I wasn't perfect, that I didn't fail, and that I can get through tough times with the help of family and friends. In the feeling, came the healing.

Depression was never something I set out to experience, but it has been the greatest life lesson.

Fiona Hurle

37

Alone, Yet Not Alone

*S*hy, unwell, isolated and misunderstood as a child; my father referred to me as *'The Cat Who Walked Alone'* – very likely a reference to the Rudyard Kipling story, The Cat that Walked by Himself. I often questioned during my early years why I had been born into my family. I really did not fit, and my parents struggled to cope with the 'strange child' they had given birth to.

Alone, although I knew I was not alone, I communicated with those who I knew around me, many of whom were deceased. My explanation of these communications were vehemently refuted by my parents and most family members with the exception of my paternal grandparents who loved, guided and understood me. Following the passing of my paternal grandfather during my seventh year, we left the United Kingdom to live on the other side of the world in East Africa. This move effectively removed the physical and emotional support of my beloved grandmother, and my continued ill health meant I was not able to attend school.

I learnt over the years to accept my physical 'aloneness' and to trust the mental communications that had been such a part of my life, especially those I related to as being from someone I identified as 'Michael'. In the late 1990s, I begrudgingly attended a one-day workshop that had been promoted by one of my metaphysical teachers and which I had avoided previously on numerous occasions.

Called 'Michael the Man, Mikael the Archangel', I was honestly sceptical; however, the quiet unassuming man dressed in white who I met before the workshop seemed pleasant and non-threatening enough, so I decided to be open to what he would share. The change of resonance, tone and pitch of Michael's voice when he allowed the energy of another to come through his body affected me more than the physical changes to his body and persona, and I was aware of a deep heart connection with him that I could not explain.

Following the workshop we spent many hours talking, as we were both staying with my teacher. We both felt comfortable sharing stories from our early lives. The following morning, Michael's partner asked me if I would like to have a private session with Mikael, the energetic being that Michael 'channelled'. I hesitated for a few moments, but some encouragement from Heather had me saying, "Yes please."

A 'Michael, Sheila is going to have a chat with Mikael,' saw Michael go and change his clothes, and the resonance of that 'different voice' called me to him. Sitting opposite Michael in his Mikael persona, I burst into tears and said, "All of my life, I have talked to someone in my head I call Michael." Reaching forward he took my hands and said, "We have known one another for a very long time, and it is how I have always communicated with you."

Asking my permission to share an energy with me, he placed his hands on my head. A sense of light, peace and fulfillment enveloped me like a wave of love. I finally understood why I had never felt alone. Driving home feeling as though I was floating above the ground, I had a permanent smile and a sense of wellbeing that has never left me. Prior to Michael's unexpected passing in the early 2000s, Mikael connected with me physically many times, intensifying our connection; he guides me still as I hold a pen to share his beautiful messages with the world.

Sheila Kennedy

38

From Misery to Inspiration

*A*fter leaving my country of birth, the place where I opened my eyes for the first time and learnt the foundation and values for my entire life, I went to Australia in search of my dreams. I could not imagine what life would offer me in my new country, based on my choices and my decisions at the time.

The worst thing that happened was not only the fact that I was abused in so many ways, but the horrible desire to harm myself to death. It felt like I placed my life in exile with my own hands. I was paralysed, and my brain was numb. I would slowly and painfully talk to myself while doing my daily routines and working for my abuser. He was keeping me under control. He had cameras installed and used to watch me all the time in the factory/workplace where I lived with him for a while. He would lock me up so that I could not go anywhere.

I was not allowed to speak or meet up with any of my friends or make new ones because everyone from his point of view was evil and could harm me. I was not allowed to speak with anyone in the workplace or anywhere else. I could not smile or be serious. If anyone was asking me something and I answered, it was a disaster. If I did not speak as I was asked, it was a disaster. The names he used to call me, and the way he abused me, were so bad you may not want to hear.

Emotionally destroyed, I found myself in desperation trying to run and escape. In my misery and my mind, that was the only way out. I was horrified at the thoughts that were running through my brain like an avalanche and wouldn't stop. It didn't matter how hard I wanted to convince myself that I could not do these horrifying things to myself and my loved ones, that it would be selfish.

They were like two powerful forces fighting with each other and destroying my entire being. I just wanted to die. I was contemplating how to do it nicely so that it won't be too scary for the people that would find me. I also thought of when my family would see the pictures; I did not want it to be so traumatising for them.

I was thinking how to make their pain much easier, but every method of doing so would've had a terrifying ending. As the years went by, my mind was so sick that I was spending full days thinking how to do it, how to come up with something new, cleaner, and not so horrible. Physically, spiritually, and mentally, I was dead. Then I thought, 'That's enough. This is unbearable. I can't stay alive, even for my family.'

I was going to make the biggest mistake on Earth. Sickened to near-death, my instincts told me not to take any more drugs from prescriptions. Instead, I would follow nature's way of healing. After two weeks of taking Australian Bush Flower Essences, the miracle finally happened. For the first time in over five years, I wanted to live again. I started fighting for my life, with a different approach and an instant thirst of life.

I don't for one second regret the things that I had to do to conquer one of the most macabre experiences. I'm grateful for everything that happened to me; I learnt a lot, it straightened me up. I became so strong and it shaped me into who I am today. It showed me how to feel and see life in a different light.

Carolina Rotaru

39

Desperation Leads to Discovery

My little dream of owning a fully managed and staffed hospitality business cracked after just two weeks, when the young and fit manager left, claiming exhaustion after just 12 months of doing about one-quarter of the work she now left me with. I was physically, mentally, and emotionally exhausted after a couple of years, but I had to keep myself going for another two until we could finally get out. Hiring, training and managing staff on the easy-going Sunshine Coast, in particular, was the hardest part of keeping things running smoothly. I was emotionally spent and all the joy of life had been squeezed out of my usually optimistic personality.

After a whole year of having several buyers refused by the franchisor, I was feeling angry, helpless, desperate, near death, totally exhausted, severely underweight and was not sleeping more than a couple of hours, waking with a start and my mind racing. I had begun to have vivid dreams of how to kill myself and soon I was feeling like the visualisations were becoming more solid and I was having trouble separating daily life from those strong thoughts. I'm sure this is how manifestation happens.

My healing moment came when I surrendered all control. Realising that I could no longer go on this way, I 'caved in' and asked for help. This was a completely new concept for me, and I woke my husband one morning in a flood of tears. I told him I could not go on and that I thought I needed to admit myself into a hospital.

I am not a medicine taker and was not willing to take as much as a headache tablet. It brings tears to my eyes when I realise how desperate I had become. It was so hard for me to admit I couldn't get myself out of this one. Bless his soul, he took me for a two-night escape by the beach where I received two massages. That was enough to reconnect with myself.

My body was the key. It was the thing that was holding me together, and it was what needed the help as my nerves were so frayed. My body had so much to teach me. I was severely underweight and my adrenals were shot. Running on empty and not resting when my body was crying out for it will do that. When I finally sold the business, I found out that my organs were on the verge of shutdown.

I began to take things seriously and made my whole life about rest, eating and sleeping whenever I needed and walking in nature. I needed to reconnect with myself on all levels. My intuition told me that my body wanted to do yoga, and I was led to Zenko yoga studio. Not only has this saved my body, but my soul has connected with like minds. It is due to connecting with the founder, Lauren Verona, that my true soul work has emerged. She helped me discover my gift of working with bodies and energy.

From wanting to get off the planet, I began to understand my role in it. I now help others to find their role and that is a gift I am grateful for every day.

My life is now filled with peace and doing things that bring me joy. I spend a lot of time in nature, realising its healing properties and importance to empathic people such as myself. I watch as my energy work changes peoples' lives, bringing them more joy and growing their businesses so that they too may share their message with the world. I travel and go away a lot, returning fresh and renewed for my clients.

Naveen Light

40

The Awakening

*A*t 18 years old, I was a college student studying to be an accountant. I had taken a precollege test that told you what career would be best for you, and accountant or park ranger showed up. I chose to go down the accounting route, even though it sounded quite dull and uninteresting at the time. I remember feeling rather lost and uninspired about school and felt I was just going through the motions.

On December 18th, 1986, I was driving to school to another uninspiring accounting class. I was running late, in a hurry and wearing no seat belt. All of a sudden, a car pulled out in front of me, leaving me no time to brake. I hit the driver's side of his car at 60 miles per hour. At impact, my head went through the windshield and I lost consciousness. I woke up several hours later in the hospital emergency room. I was in a lot of pain with bruises, a broken finger and with severe injuries to my neck and shoulder. The doctors were amazed that I had not broken my neck, been paralysed or killed.

Later that day, the doctor came in to my room and said, "Okay Dave, you can go." With a puzzled look, I replied, "But wait Doc, I can't move my neck or my shoulder. What do I need to do?" He then proceeded to hand me three prescriptions and told me to take the pills and I should be fine afterwards. I looked at the prescription and over at my parents with a confused expression. At this point in my life, I had no education on health and healing, but I knew that this did not make sense.

I elected not to take the pills and, with the advice from my parents, I decided to give chiropractic a try. When I went to the office, my pain was excruciating and I had little to no movement in my neck or shoulder. I was a bit apprehensive but was willing to try anything at this point.

After a thorough examination, the chiropractor had me lie down on the treatment table. At that moment I did not realise that the next thing he was going to do would change my life forever. He gently put his hands on my neck and gave me my first chiropractic adjustment.

When I got off the table it was like a miracle. Instantly, most of my pain was gone and I could move my neck and shoulder once again. I was amazed! I asked the doctor, "What did you just do to me?"

He sat me down and explained to me about chiropractic and healing. It made complete sense to me and could feel a transformation in myself. In that moment, I saw a vision of what I was here to do. I had just been awakened to my mission in life. I was to become a chiropractor and share this gift with others.

The next day, with extreme delight, I dropped my accounting classes and began my quest to be a doctor of chiropractic. It was later in life when I began to learn and teach about universal laws and divine order that I understood just how important that so called 'accident' and near death experience was to my journey. It was the most important event in my life that set me on my path of healing and self-discovery.

Our greatest blessings arise out of our biggest challenges. Have gratitude for yourself and your life.

Dave Tuck

41

Seeing Beyond Fears

One minute I was riding around in the arena having fun, the next minute the pony took off.

I remember the adults around me yelling at me to hold on, but it was too late. The reins had been ripped out of my hands and my feet slipped out of the stirrups. I tried to reach for the reins to pull him up, but it was too late. I was flying through the air before I landed on the top of my head and flipped onto my back. Me being me, I thought I was fine; I stood straight up and tried to walk over to the adults, almost crashing into a horse jump in the process. Little did I know that moment would change my life as I knew it!

Fast-forward two years. Things had taken a turn for the worse. I was unable to be at school so I had dropped out and started online school. I loved it, I but was still struggling with understanding my work. It was very frustrating to me, as I had been an A-student.

I was feeling very judged by everyone: my teachers at my old school, my friends and even my family. I felt alone, insecure, and it made me question all of my decisions. I started getting these weird attacks, my vision would black out, my ears started ringing and I was unable to stand up. We went to the doctor's, but no one could figure out what the attacks were, so they just put it down to anxiety.

Later we found a new doctor who, within asking me a few basic questions, knew something wasn't right. She sent me to a behavioural optometrist, where I found out that I had suffered a brain injury from the fall, resulting in Post-Traumatic Vision Syndrome (PTVS). I was told I would need 20 weeks of vision therapy at a minimum, as well as craniosacral therapy to help with the physical aspect. I was so happy that we finally found out what was wrong and why I struggled with school.

I started vision therapy as well as cranio, but my body couldn't cope with it all. I was bedridden for six weeks, unable to stand without my vision going. I only left the house to go to therapy sessions; I had to stop school for the year, which frustrated me beyond belief. I was scared that it was doing the opposite of what it was supposed to and that I wouldn't get better. I just wanted to be a teenager and have fun; I was sick of my life being run by my injury. In that moment I knew I had to continue if I wanted my life to get better.

I worked hard at vision therapy and temporarily stopped the craniosacral therapy. I was starting to feel more like myself and was coping better. The most important thing I learnt in vision therapy was about looking hard or soft.

If I'm looking 'hard' at everything, my body is tense and my peripheral vision doesn't work; but if I looked 'soft', I was more relaxed and I could see everything around me. I noticed small improvements towards the end of the 20 weeks. That was when I was told that since my vision is so sensitive, I would need one to two more years of vision therapy, as we needed to take things slow.

So, I decided I needed a break, time to just be a teenager. We agreed that I would start again in six months, so I have chosen to spend that time getting over my fear of horses. I don't want to be afraid anymore. I want to ride again.

Elina Passant

42

Fear of Rejection

A few years ago my life was blown apart. I was going through a tough time in my life and some things people did cut me deeply to my core, even though I knew in all of my heart that I was doing all I could in the circumstances. As a result, the extreme stress and trauma took its toll on my health and well-being.

During this time, I went to bed one night feeling fine and woke up the next morning coughing and not able to breathe. How did that happen? This was my second bout with severe pneumonia in two years and I knew I was in trouble. The experience had left me physically, mentally, and emotionally bankrupt – there was no reserve left at all. I felt completely vulnerable and unprotected.

Over the past six years, there had been a constant run of challenging events, this last one being the worst. I had broken off a long-term significant relationship and experienced my first bout of pneumonia through the life-threatening illness of psittacosis. Then, estrangement with my family of origin, theft of a horse that was gifted to my daughter, and finally my daughter getting bucked off a pony and landing on her head, which resulted in an undiagnosed brain injury.

All these experiences contained a familiar thread that was running throughout my life – chaos, trauma and grief (in Chinese Medicine, grief sits in the lungs). Looking deeper to see what my behaviours were trying to show me, I realised that I was in survival mode again! Then, the greatest realisation then slammed down on me – my whole life has been in survival mode and trauma was the key.

Soul Healer, Simone Engdahl, encouraged me to go even deeper beyond traditional healing methods to understand the trauma in the collective soul of our family. On investigation, I found there had been many unresolved hidden family secrets and traumas. The pain body or collective shadow gets passed down through the family, just like DNA.

At Simone's suggestion, I sat down in meditation and called all my ancestors to join me. I asked, 'What needs to be healed that has not been spoken about?' With all those answers, I was able to acknowledge their fears and traumas, then hand back the bundle of shared pain to them. In doing so, I began the healing of our family soul.

It was in that divine moment I finally understood why it had been so difficult for me to change my life circumstances. The inherited codependency conditioning was so deeply ingrained. Through a lot of investigation, I was able to see how dysfunctional my normal way of being really was and how it affected every aspect of my life. Being hypervigilant, walking on eggshells around people, not rocking the boat or expressing my views in fear of being rejected—all of these happened on a regular basis in my family.

Over the years, I had attracted toxic love interests, and friends whom I felt blindsided by. The biggest and most recent message of all was feeling completely judged by the outside world in my ability to take care of my daughter.

Now it is completely different. Finally, I have woken up and can clearly see when my wounded adult child is going into survival mode, and I can reclaim my power. The times when I get triggered, and begin to feel invisible or unworthy, is when I know to step up my self-care. Chaos is now my ladder that leads me back to my wholeness, to self-love, and my valuing all of who I am.

Heather Passant

43

Loving Life Through the Soul

J was a teacher working my way up the leadership ladder, loving teaching and all the challenges that went with it. But I began to feel disheartened with the education industry and felt a calling to make a change and create something. So I left teaching to pursue an entrepreneurial journey as an education consultant. I thought this would be easy, being a teacher and having firsthand knowledge of the problems schools face...boy was I wrong! What I didn't realise was how much being an entrepreneur made you step outside of your comfort zone. I felt naked, with no mask of an organisation to hide behind.

I was being judged on how I looked, how I spoke, and what qualifications I had. I felt vulnerable, which was something I was not used to. This feeling of being judged, unworthy, and not enough had a huge impact on how the rest of my education consultant journey went. I failed. My confidence dropped, and I began to shy away from the people I most wanted to help. I felt like a failure to my husband, who had sacrificed himself to be our family's sole income earner so I could follow my dream. I felt useless.

One day my son asked, "So how is your business going, Mum?" In that moment, my heart sank and I realised that my children were also watching my journey. I did not want them to see me give up. I replied to him with a loving smile, "It's not good, son, I need to do lots of work on me."

This was the turning point and the birth of my soul development (personal development for the soul). I had invested a lot of money into knowing the craft of business and the expertise of business coaches, but what was missing was the craft of knowing exactly who I was, and to honour that above all.

I attended a 'Feminine Business Leadership Training'. During this workshop, I was introduced to a meditation technique that blew my mind wide open. This was the first time I had felt energy this intense!

I continued to meditate and connect my entire body to this intense powerful energy over the course of the workshop, and I could feel a huge shift surge within my body; somewhere deep but I couldn't pinpoint where. After working with this energy for three days, the fourth day required we complete speaking training. I got up on the stage and began my business pitch, "Hi, I'm Delvina, and…" I stopped dead in my tracks. I could hear what was going on in the heads of the audience. I could hear what they were thinking! This scared the crap out of me that I couldn't go on. In fact, I burst into tears. How embarrassing.

What just happened? Divine guidance told me I was experiencing communication of the soul. I was experiencing the soul truth of others. During the three days of meditation and feeling into my own intense energy, I was in fact connecting to my soul…or my soul was re-connecting to my entire being. This pure soul connection allowed me to connect to others on a soul-level. I could see and feel their true feelings even though they were telling me something different.

This experience changed my life. The deeper connection to my soul has made the relationships with my husband, children and family more fulfilling. I feel worthy of every bit of happiness and success that comes my way because I finally feel like I am enough. I have returned to teaching and have a different view on how I will make a difference in the world.

Delvina Waiti

44

Heal Your Life

*G*rowing up with domestic violence and parents who were not very loving, I developed some deep seated fears. Life at primary school was unpleasant as I was bullied severely by my so-called 'friends' and even my teacher was a bully. During those unhappy years my joy was connecting to my creativity in creating characters, writing and producing plays.

After my parents separated in 1976 my life settled. By 1979, I was so much happier, especially after meeting and falling madly in love with my first boyfriend. In the 4 years were we together we were inseparable. I felt so blessed to have such a fabulous boyfriend who I loved with all my heart.

Unfortunately, my fears really came into play just prior to my 18th birthday when I decided that, even though we were both in love and there was talk of marriage, I felt I could not stay with him. The marriage part was extremely scary to me, having witnessed my parents unloving marriage, so I sadly ended the relationship. I broke both our hearts and I believe this was the catalyst for my first nervous breakdown.

At the age of 20, after ending another two-year relationship and resigning from my job, I decided on a whim to move to Sydney. With the stress of moving and feeling quite isolated, I had another nervous breakdown. This time it was severe as I even contemplated suicide and knew I needed professional help. Upon seeing a psychiatrist and confessing my suicidal thoughts, I was immediately admitted into a private psychiatric clinic, for two weeks and heavily medicated.

I returned to work and quickly realised that I could not continue the same amount of medication as I was literally walking around like a zombie. No longer suicidal, I reduced my medication each day to the point I didn't need any. I truly believe that utilising a few key principles enabled me to heal myself naturally. This included not drinking alcohol, getting 8 hours sleep and filling my body with nutrients and natural supplements.

My recovery was exceptional, however I felt lonely and decided to return to my home town and continue with my healthy lifestyle determined to rebuild my life once again. It was at this time that I discovered several books on personal development that would help change my mindset and consequently my life. One book that had a significant effect on me was *The Power of the Spoken Word* by Florence Scovel-Shinn. I began to implement the key strategies of utilising the power of our minds and the powerful principles of affirmations and visualisations.

As I began to see the results I realised just how powerful our minds were. My life became more abundant and I started to feel amazing in mind, body, and soul. I read other books like *You Can Heal Your Life* by Louise Hay which enabled me to also work on self-love. I soon found that I no longer suffered mental illness and I started to love my life and found that life loved me right back.

I was to encounter many other challenges and some harsh lessons, but I had no more 'episodes' and remained mentally well. My personal development work continues to this day and improving my self-love has been a huge journey. I realised that no matter what we go through in life we need to be truly accountable and take charge. We all have the capacity to create a life that is truly magnificent if we invest in becoming a better version of ourselves, heal from the past and love ourselves a little more each day, I believe that's when the true 'miracles' occur

Jo Worthy

45

Self-Love Saved My Life

asping for life and experiencing severe abdominal convulsions, left me gripping onto the cold metal kitchen sink, with my body swaying uncontrollably from side to side. Desperately, I kept trying to find my balance.

Living alone in my apartment meant I had no one to help me. Mustering the little strength that I had left, I clutched onto the kitchen sink to keep me from collapsing and striking my head onto the hard kitchen floor. Oscillating between deep dizziness and vertigo, my free hand was desperately reaching towards my mobile phone in my frantic, fumbling attempt to call the emergency line.

All of my significant sensory systems were now failing me. I panicked! I somehow leapt from the kitchen sink with my phone in hand, directly to my bed, as fast as I could. Somehow I found the strength to finally unlock my mobile phone and dial the emergency number (000 in Australia).

'Thank God!' I thought. The ambulance was on its way. I lay on my soon-to-be deathbed and began hearing the loud piercing sounds of the ambulance siren outside. Blaring and deafening, my ears jumped into hypersensitivity. I kept thinking this one is literally for ME! With the last ounce of energy that I had left within me, I crawled, struggled and staggered to open the door for the ambulance paramedic team to arrive. 'They are here', I thought.

I was in a semi-conscious state, somewhat weak and lifeless, but breathing. I was placed onto an ambulance stretcher, still holding onto my bucket for dear life, constantly expelling the excess bile and remaining contents of my now empty stomach. As I was being lifted into the ambulance, I caught a glimpse of myself in its tinted reflective windows, and thought to myself, 'Who is this?.'

I felt deeply unrecognisable. I had suddenly changed from my beautiful peaches and cream complexion to a now deeply jaundiced shade of mustard yellow from head to toe - the whites of my eyes included and I was uncontrollably scratching my skin until it bled.

In the cold corridor of the hospital wing I remained waiting, waiting for my partner who never came. I felt deeply abandoned, afraid and alone. Time passed so slowly, each minute felt like an hour. Finally, after much anxiety and anticipation, I was being wheeled into the liver transplant unit, ICU. What began to unfold before my very eyes was beyond my comprehension.

I was being informed by surgeons that I was in fact now dying and it was a race against time to save my life! Doctors, nurses, surgeons, catheters, permacaths, vials, machines, tubes, and syringes now covered me from chest to legs. I was being prodded and poked all over. My inner voice trembled with fear, yet I had an intuitive knowing that I would still survive. I sensed that my body would miraculously heal itself.

I refused liver transplantation and placed my faith in me. I received plasma exchange and practiced my secrets to self-love daily. I am proud to say that after my one-month battle for life in the ICU, and against all medical expectations, I became a world first miracle survivor to have lived through a very rare liver condition known as Wilson's disease. I am a living, loving, breathing miracle.

Why do I believe in miracles again? Because I am one!

Vas Bes

46

Let Go of Negative Energies

My problems began when I developed environment illness at 20 years old. I was like the boy in the bubble spending one Canadian winter with the windows open because I couldn't breathe in the fumes from the heater. I also had chronic fatigue, weighing just 54kg at one point.

There were emotional events too. The first girl I ever loved cheated on me. I was crushed because I had really trusted her. And so, the journey of looking into improving myself started when I was 20. I've also had the experience of two toxic relationships.

I often felt a universal force speaking to me, saying, 'Young man, you're going to have to get over yourself or I'm going to make this really, really painful for you'—although I didn't hear it the first two or three times. I had feelings of shame, resentment, and anger that pushed me to go figure out this emotional stuff and see whoever I needed to and do whatever I needed to get clear. I was really committed.

Emotional Freedom Technique reduced my anxiety, but did not give me the peace, calm, and balance I craved. I tried other modalities, including bioenergetics, NLP, hypnosis, spiritual healings, and energetic healings. I had heard of emotional clearing, but it didn't sound like something I wanted to do. I got to a state of desperation. It came down to the fact that I had tried everything else, so I might as well try that. It was very emotionally painful, slow and like an onion with 20 layers I'd peel off two or three layers knowing there was many more to go.

I thought there had to be a better way. I just wanted to pull out the core of it taking all the layers with it. If the body innately uses the nervous system to transport emotions through the body and mind, it made sense that we would remove the emotions the same way. I wondered how I would get these emotions I was holding, to bolt out of the nervous system, out of the cells, and leave my body through my skin.

My mind was like that of a 'mad scientist', mixing and combining elements of 'this' from the chiropractors and 'that' from the tantra people and 'this' from the emotional clearing and blending them into a simple usable formula that would work. I had a real sense of urgency with it, as I had already exhausted so much time, energy and money.

At home I sat on the sofa and by unpacking all of these little nuances that were coming to me and threading it together over a period of about two and a half hours, I pieced it together. IT WORKED. I literally felt it coming out of my skin. When that first happened to me, it changed everything. I felt emotionally clear. I stood taller. My eyes were brighter. For the first time, I knew what emotional calm was.

Your perfect life shows up out of unanticipated circumstances. You can't plan it. All you can do is try to free up the energy that allows it to come to you in a more profound and expedited way.

I'm proof. The clearer I get, the more life flows.

From speaking alongside Richard Branson, adopting our son from Vanuatu, loving my partner more deeply, creating a seven-figure business, and most recently my success with affiliate marketing; it all just began to flow for me. It is all about becoming more and more emotionally clear. I feel 'ever-expanded' as a human being as a result of emotional clearing. I now teach the technique, at no charge, to any entrepreneur who wants to also find emotional harmony. It's my way of giving back.

Shaune Clarke

47

Healing from Chronic Fatigue

J had always been an extremely active person; but after having a draining cold for four weeks, I was physically drained – I was tired to the bone and my core was exhausted. The doctor called it 'chronic fatigue' and it sounded as horrible as it was.

I was unable to move from the corpse position for three months whilst my husband, mother, and children looked after me. All I had was my will and my mind, as my body felt dead. My positive thoughts and healing visions helped me keep myself alive.

I was still tired four years later – everyday I was hardly able to drag my feet and body around. I had come to accept it by allocating many sleep times during my day and taking really good care of myself. Somehow I knew I had the power to get through this. I knew things would change. After using the guidance from the GPs and still feeling exhausted, I tried many modalities, vitamins, herbs, and alternative healing to boost me up, but to no avail.

I eventually came across an amazing facilitator. He invited me to come for a session called 'The Process', which I had never heard of. It was a new experience for me. I had to trust myself, my instincts and look inside my body – I felt it was a crazy idea. We began by taking a journey sensing into my body via observations, listening, and feeling. There was no life force in my body or my aura.

By following the process of searching inside myself, I was able to identify many layers or parts of me that needed healing. Through my acknowledgment of what I found, I was able to heal the parts inside me that needed healing.

I can't describe them all here as many such things took place during this one session; but one that was most significant was when I looked into my heart and saw a black object there with the shape of the liver. As I looked closer, it looked like a heavy black shiny crystal called obsidian; when I looked closer again, I saw that it had lines on it. The lines became white fingers. At that point, I looked at the arms that belonged to the fingers, it was then I realised that these fingers came from angels who were taking this big black thing out of me. I can't describe the feeling as I handed over this big weight that felt like it had been inside me for many years – the relief, the gratitude.

Again I followed the guidance looking deeper into the space that was inside me as we moved through many blockages like this. At the end I felt exhausted, but somehow amazing, I knew then that something had changed.

I went straight to bed, and lay there thinking that I had just been through something amazing. As I lay there, a small gold ball came into my body. It buzzed throughout my whole body as fast as the speed of light; it seemed to be energising my body. It spun so fast that I was feeling incredible, filled with light, love and energy. I fell into a deep sleep, and awoke several hours later knowing that I was going to be ok.

From that day, I gradually became stronger.

Ten years later, deep gratitude still radiates from my heart. I knew then that one day I was going to be facilitating this process for others with my intuitive healing work with the light.

Jennie de Vine

48

Creativity: A Path to Wellness

My left arm had developed a frozen shoulder. It was April 2014, and I was in constant pain. I felt like a bird with a broken wing.

When it became overwhelming and debilitating, my medical doctor friend said, "We don't know why it comes on, but it seems to sort itself out in one to two years." The voice in my head screamed, "I can't put up with this for another week let alone two years!"

I had strained my shoulder lifting my handbag from the back to the front seat while driving! In the months following, the pain increased and my shoulder gradually lost mobility – I could barely lift my arm. I became more and more miserable and exhausted with chronic pain. I was unable to sleep and even driving became a struggle. Just before I injured my shoulder, my mum had died of cancer. My anguish at her loss and the stress of a conflict with my stepfather took me to my lowest ebb.

I began using EFT (tapping) to process all the built up emotions of grief and anger. I consulted a doctor who claimed to be the only practitioner in Australia who had success with frozen shoulders. I spoke with him about his procedure, and he proposed to pump my shoulder with cortisone injections and then perform a rapid manoeuvre that would tear the scar tissue apart. The thought of causing MORE trauma to my shoulder made me felt physically ill. I knew that way wasn't for me.

I sensed, saw, and felt back to meditation. I journeyed deep within my body and sensed/saw/felt into my injured arm. I followed that with artwork - a body mapping process - to capture the emotions, colours and textures I perceived residing there - hot, spiky, dark, feeling responsible and carrying a huge weighty burden. I then drew my body and focused on all the feelings, sensations and words I wanted to feel in my shoulder- gratitude for the returned strength, ease and mobility of my shoulder, a glowing beam of green, blue and gold.

One day, I had a breakthrough in my awareness. It was like a whole body of reckoning hit me as I went to move the position of my left arm - a huge wave of fear rose up!

The panic I had dwelling in my shoulder was almost overwhelming. It was mine. It was my mother who I knew was very afraid of dying. I then had a flash of me sitting on the edge of her bed as she was taking her last breaths. I had been holding her hand in my left hand. In the moment of strong connection that existed between us as she died, I held onto some of her energy, fear, and distress. And that was magnified by my own grief and loss.

From the moment, I had that opening in my awareness, I was able to heal. I continued to do energy clearing work using tapping and meditation. In the coming days and weeks, my shoulder got rapidly and noticeably more mobile and less painful. Within one month, I was back to about 75% function – I could lift my arm above shoulder height again and do up my bra as I would normally. I could get comfortable and sleep soundly.

I found this quote at the time and have kept it with the drawings I did, "The truth is that our finest moments are most likely to occur when we are feeling deeply uncomfortable, unhappy, or unfulfilled. For it is only in such moments, propelled by our discomfort, that we are likely to step out of our ruts and start searching for different ways or truer answers." – M. Scott Peck

Michelle Walker

49

Accept and Turn Situations Around

J left behind a stressful corporate world for a life of fun, travel, and adventure. After three years of travelling around Australia, I found my paradise on the Sunshine Coast. I began living my dreams and became a successful photojournalist, publishing five books. Life was fabulous.

Then, on Christmas Eve 2014, my husband, Greg, had an emergency quadruple bypass. Waiting in intensive care, I felt a familiar wave of fear resurface. I lost my previous partner to cancer and I was scared that I would lose Greg too. Thankfully, Greg survived.

A lot was going on in my life while he was in hospital, and I was desperately trying to convince myself I was fine. Who was I trying to kid? I was really not coping. One morning I woke up with an excruciating pain in my feet. My bones were screaming at me when I walked. It felt like a bee sting with a burning sensation. I was scared and saw a doctor that day. I was sent to get blood tests, which revealed rheumatoid arthritis. My immune system was attacking the lining of my joints. Treatment is typically methotrexate, a chemotherapy drug.

No thanks, not an option for me, especially not after seeing what my previous partner went though. Over the next 12 months, I completed a detox, eliminating gluten, dairy, grains, and nightshade foods from my diet. I also tried a multitude of anti-inflammatory supplements, but I saw no improvement. I struggled with the reality of my future life, crippled with rheumatoid arthritis and suffering permanent excruciating pain. Severely depressed and defeated, I succumbed and began taking methotrexate.

It gave me brain fog, a nasty rash, and a constant feeling of nausea. I felt miserable and helpless, thinking this was how my life would be. A friend told me about her husband who has ankylosing spondylitis – inflammatory arthritis of the spine. She mentioned he was having a positive results by activating his Nrf2 pathway, which triggers a biochemical wakeup call at a cellular level repairing damaged cells and reducing pain and inflammation in the body. I tried it...call it gut instinct. 'What if it works?'

I noticed a gradual reduction in pain. Within three weeks, I stopped taking Nurofen and even slept through the night. I continued yoga and meditation even if just to roll out the mat, lay in Child's Pose and just be. Without pain, I had more clarity and began to reflect on my situation.

It was during yoga Nidra when I asked the universe for guidance, 'Where's the lesson in this? What are you trying to tell me?' It was that moment when I realised what I needed to do: trust my own intuition and not listen to everyone else. I had to accept the diagnosis and listen to what my fragile body was trying to tell me. How ironic. I knew stress fed this disease, but I was stressed out while trying everything I could to control it. I stopped trying to 'fix' myself and focused on having faith that activating my body's own immune system and reducing inflammation would help me mindfully surrender to the healing process my body was asking for.

Within 16 months, I went from needing help showering and not being able to cut my food to being totally medication-free. I've even started yoga and my general physical and mental health is bouncing back more each month. I am back doing what I love - photojournalism and spending time with my friends, family and grandchildren.

Helga Dalla

50

The Piano

*E*verything changed the moment my childhood piano was sold.

It was November 2015, and I was so angry; it felt like a line had been drawn in the sand and the universe had closed the door on me ever becoming a musician. I hadn't touched the piano in a decade, but I had always thought it would be there when I was ready.

2013 was the year that my life as I knew it ended. I was suffering from a myriad of autoimmune disease symptoms and had gone from a slim size eight to an inflamed size 14 in five months. I had digestive issues plus regular migraines, joint pain, brain fog, body rashes, extreme fatigue, and anxiety and depression. I no longer felt myself.

No one could tell me what was happening; I just kept getting sicker. Three different doctors said nothing was wrong, while another one said that I was just depressed and 'eating my feelings'.

I was struggling intensely with inhabiting a larger body. I felt like my overall worth had somehow decreased. It became clear that I had been experiencing body dysmorphia long before this, and these longstanding issues were rising to the surface. There were days and weeks where I hated myself because of the size of my body. It makes my blood boil and my heart cry, because this body-image beast affects almost every woman I speak to.

I had fully immersed myself in a 'quarter life crisis' which involved sleeping and binge watching television. For a few months, it seemed like all I could do; my symptoms were preventing me from normal functioning. Eventually I found a good doctor and started treatment for early stage autoimmune symptoms, thyroid issues, and adrenal fatigue. I started on supplements and my symptoms started to improve. Concurrently, I did intensive internal work that addressed a range of things from my body image, my inner people pleaser, and my highly active self-critic. I also found self-love through this process. But I should say that none of this was quick or painless. It felt like every small step took forever. Two years later, just as I was starting to heal and my childhood piano was sold, I bought my own antique piano from Gumtree. It turned out that I was not okay with giving up on myself as a musician.

In the following 18 months, I took action, including music coaching, singing lessons, and song writing. I auditioned for and performed in an amateur musical and started performing at local markets and a women's festival. I studied the music business and started sharing my music online. Most importantly, I started calling myself a musician.

I had been unconsciously living the life of a people-pleaser, a rat stuck in a wheel, going round and round in circles, getting frustrated that life wasn't going to plan. But did I magically stop people pleasing, lose 30 kg, regain full health, and become a famous musician? Well, actually, no, this is not that story.

I took supplements, worked on my inner self, sang and created. I worked hard, and I continue to do all of these things. While I am mostly healthy now, a symptom flare up happens every now and again. The extra weight is coming off very, very slowly, and self-love is a daily practice. I am still getting clarity on my future direction, and where I want to take my music. In short, big incredible life changes have happened, but I am a work in progress. Watch this space.

Elysia Anketell

51

The Power of Prayer

*M*y life changed on that fateful day in January 1954 when Dad found mum slumped on the floor with the smell of gas emanating from the gas oven. I was three weeks old. It was difficult for Dad to raise a newborn as a widower while looking after his two other daughters. So, he found a loving family to adopt me into their home. The pain of neglect I felt at that time was hard to endure, and I was hit by a wave of sadness and isolation.

Six months later I was back with my dad and sisters. It was a very unsettling time as I struggled to adapt to my stepmother and stepsiblings while reuniting with my two sisters at the same time. I felt anxious, like a stranger in my own family; I was very confused.

12 months later, my half-sister was born, and that was the beginning of my Cinderella experience. Dad decided to migrate to Australia. The journey by ship from Holland was long and arduous. I cried on that voyage, feeling insecure, lost, and alone, craving love and attention.

Wearing secondhand clothes during my childhood and teenage years made me feel embarrassed. I worried what other kids would think of me and did my best to hide to avoid judgement and criticism. I truly believed there was something wrong with me, and I couldn't understand why I was being treated differently to my younger sister. I didn't feel good about myself and perceived my life as hell. I would hear voices in my head affirming, 'You are useless and no good to anybody', and experience pain and tension in my neck and shoulders. I lacked energy and constantly felt tired.

At 20, I married—only to discover 11 years later that I was not the only woman in my husband's life. I divorced and fell in and out of failed relationships. Depression set in – I just wanted to die.

It wasn't until my mid 30s when I reflected on my failed marriage and relationships. I felt anxious and afraid of being on my own for the rest of my life. I started to pray. I asked God for help.

Something inside guided me to walk into the personal development section of a bookstore where the book, *You Can Heal Your Life*, by Louise Hay jumped out at me. That was the turning point of my life. I read the book and was relieved to discover that thoughts can be changed. I was inspired by Louise's ability to overcome her physical and mental abuse. A new sense of hope returned, and I diligently followed the workbook and changed my pattern of thinking.

That led me to attend many spiritual and personal development workshops whereupon I returned to love discovering that it was always there. It was my illusive thoughts that steered me away from love.

I changed my thinking, which led me to develop long-term relationships and understand life's challenges. I learnt to live in the present and appreciate each moment. I meditated daily to return to a state of calm, which helped relieve my tension and anxiety. I developed a routine of walking daily and spending time in nature to uplift my energy and feel better about myself.

In Dr Demartini's Breakthough Experience I dissolved resentment and anger towards my stepmum, and adopted 'Holy Spirit' into my life for comfort, love, and security. I am eternally grateful to God for guiding and assisting me with grace to overcome the pain of depression and rejection. I am happily married to the man of my dreams and most importantly, give thanks that my prayers were answered.

Jackie Mortimer

52

The Gift of Surrender

*D*espite appearances of being a self-aware, strong woman, I felt 'wrong' for most of my life. My self-doubt was behind almost every choice I'd made from the age of 15 setting me on the path to an eventual breakdown.

I was a divorced single mum and, despite efforts to change my life, I was in a constant struggle to survive. The insistent pressures of raising a family on my own and what felt like unrelenting attempts by others to derail me – as a woman of integrity and as a mother – spiralled me towards total breakdown. I lost the capacity to concentrate and manage day-to-day tasks. I couldn't be around people; I procrastinated over everything and made excuses to stay indoors. Anxiety became my constant state. Suicidal thoughts became a daily occurrence until one day when I realised I had cried every day for over a year. I was no longer the vivacious, energetic, lovable woman I used to be.

I was diagnosed with PTSD, depression, and anxiety; but I had grown up in a home where mental illness was the boss, and it was not going to be the boss of me. The symptoms were real, but labels and band-aid treatments weren't going to help me.

It was on the floor of the shower, sobbing and feeling totally alone, that I had a profound realisation – no one was coming. No one was going to save me. Changing my life was an inside job. My tenacity still burned and I knew that to change this, I had to go within – deeper than I ever had before. I had to be broken open so that I could rebuild a new sense of self.

Adrenal fatigue, exhaustion, defeat, anger, and resentment had brought me to a place of absolute surrender. From that place, I began to let go of the weight of the belief that I was incapable and that I wasn't enough. I could no longer carry those beliefs if I wanted to survive. After a lifetime of believing that I was innately 'wrong', I realised that no amount of external validation was going to set me free.

The turning point was in the surrender and in making the choice for something greater for my life. Kindness to myself was the first step and the most difficult. With a full-blown nervous breakdown imminent, I began the most profound journey back to me. This experience was a pivotal point in my growth in consciousness. It took courage and vulnerability and it was tough; but with no energy left to resist, I was broken wide open. There was not one part of who I was that wasn't exposed. I began a regime of supplements, good nutrition, gentle exercise, and journaling – lots of journaling – and my health improved. I had more energy and I began to feel a sense of hope.

The key to healing was in the surrender. When I stopped trying to hang on by my teeth, the space was provided for change. When I was willing to put down old beliefs, I received a glimpse of my future self and I began to trust her. And I began to love her. Life is still challenging and the journey to healing continues.

Two years on, I am studying at university to become a psychologist and working in a job that I love. I am no longer crippled by the opinions of others. I know I'm a good mum because it is reflected through the strong, kind people my children are becoming.

Every experience is designed to make you greater, not smaller. Everything is a gift to help you expand into the full expression of who you are. I truly do believe that brilliance exists in every one of us.

Nicole Taryn

53

Remembering Mom

My mom was my person. She was my first phone call when I needed to share something. I always felt safe and loved. She is one of 15 children of whom seven have died from, or currently have, Alzheimer's disease. I know it sounds crazy, right?

Mom was a real estate broker, the best in town and even became a member of the Million Dollar Club for real estate sales, a big deal in the 80s. She worked from sunup till sundown helping people get a mortgage for a home they could raise their families in. She married young, had four children, and divorced her abusive husband. She was always independent, telling me to get my own career so I wouldn't have to rely on a man. I used to joke with mom, that when she was old, I would 'stick' her in a nursing home. She would say, "You better not." Little did I know!

At first, it was calls from the office; she hadn't shown up for an appointment or had forgotten items on contracts. She was the one who made decisions about her life. It wasn't my place to tell her what to do. She knew what to do, didn't she? Can't she see she was forgetting things? No, she could not. What was I supposed to do with this information? My gut knew what was going on. 'Please don't force me to make decisions about Mom', I prayed.

One day she called me saying she couldn't remember how to get to our house. When she became confused about how to get home from a church convention that she had attended every year, I knew I had to get out of my denial and help her. I was heavily relied on to figure this all out as the medical person in the family. How could I do that when I was grieving along with everyone else, and just wanted this diagnosis of Alzheimer's to go away? So, in my 30s, attending grad school and with two children of my own, I moved my mom in with us. I was too young to be having these experiences – too young to be losing my best friend.

I was a walking anxiety attack. I had minimal respite. I came to the realisation that I was not able to give her what she needed. After five months I made the painful decision to move her into assisted living. I constantly doubted if I made the right decision. I was frequently on the phone making sure she was okay. I had felt helpless many times through this illness. I wanted to make it all okay for her, to stop the progression of the disease. I needed more time with her.

Then she wandered outside the facility, so she was not safe there anymore and needed long-term care. That move was, without a doubt, the hardest part for me. I felt like she didn't even know I was there. This was one hard pill to swallow. The denial that stayed with me had to go. The knots in my stomach were big.

When my anxiety got completely out of control and I was unable to work, I realised I needed to start healing from the loss of my relationship with my mom as I knew it.

I sought mental health counselling, and spent a lot of time in prayer. My church was my comfort and as time went on I realised I needed to make something good out of this awful experience. I involved myself in the Alzheimer's Association and yearly walk to end the disease. I took a course on facilitating monthly support groups to help those experiencing the same challenges.

I'm stronger than I thought I was – you were right, Mom!

Christine Di Leone

54

The Power of Self-Transformation

*S*everal years ago, after having my three children and raising them to a point where they were no longer totally dependent on me, I began to feel that I had forgotten who I was. I had certainly changed during that time due to being a mother, but who I truly was had become a mystery to me.

I found myself yearning for new and exciting experiences and felt I needed a change in my career. I decided to attend a seminar for entrepreneurs. I hadn't really thought of myself as entrepreneurial, but working in the creative field for over 20 years had provided me with the skills to work on designing my own path. I listened intently as the speaker at the seminar explained how long-held belief systems are passed down to us but that we have a choice in changing how we see ourselves. I realised that to pursue a new path, I needed to focus first on my own self-awareness and healing.

To regain confidence and pursue my passions, I needed to work on myself to overcome the fears and self-doubt I had held onto for most of my life. This self-doubt was exacerbated when I became a parent.

My feelings of 'not being enough' had led me to neglect my health – particularly my mental health and wellbeing. Our family had also recently experienced trauma with the passing of several close family members. I had experienced sadness early in my life at age nine when my parents divorced and then pursued new relationships. My mind was a rollercoaster of emotions, and I often felt out of control. I began to experience anxiety. It was time to face these challenges and overcome the sadness I was feeling inside.

Soon after making this decision, I met a person who would become my coach. My coach always said to me, "there are no coincidences". I believe he came into my life at the perfect time. I soon realised through my coaching sessions that I was going through a transformational experience. I awoke to the realisation of my true self, that over time

I had come to believe I wasn't good enough but I had the power to transform into the person I wanted to be. I was unaware I was letting my ego control me. I learnt a very powerful concept of consciousness and taking control of my thoughts, feelings, and actions. I also discovered how to put this into practice every day.

Egos comprise our desires, psychological states, and behavioural patterns that we assume make us who we are. When we succumb to desires and let our egos control us, we become the opposite of who we are. We are no longer in control or in a conscious state.

It was a simple concept I hadn't learnt before, and I soon realised that, the more conscious I became of myself, my thoughts, and how I reacted in different situations, the more I was able to see the true me and be the person I wanted to be. It was a very difficult process to go through – looking inwards at both my strengths and weaknesses, but it was an experience that helped me to find inner peace.

The methods I learnt in being conscious and in the moment are skills I must practice everyday. The impact on my happiness and that of my family has been life changing. We have a happier home, as I am more calm, considered, aware, and intentional in my parenting. This has also affected everyone around me. I have increased my confidence and courage and am no longer afraid of who I am and what I have to offer. I understand fear and how it can prevent me from becoming who I am truly meant to be and how I can help others.

Rachel Saliba

55

The Power to Choose

$\mathcal{J}$'d always wanted to take a year off and travel. There was just something about the freedom of not having to be anywhere by a certain time. I'd been constantly putting it off for years. I travelled each year taking time off work but I wanted to travel for a longer time: a year.

Career is so important, I'd tell myself. Wait until I have enough money or I've paid the house off, or even, wait until I retire. Any time I really wanted something, I'd always talk myself out of it. A new camera? I wanted it but do I really need it? 'No', I would tell myself. From the outside, people thought I was fine. I had a great job, an awesome career, and I was in a loving relationship, but something was missing. I felt trapped inside this life I'd fallen into with seemingly no way out.

The doctor could never tell me why I was experiencing regular chest pains. I'd been twice, reporting that it felt like someone had punched me in centre of the chest, but both times, they had no idea what it was, assuring me it wasn't a heart attack. They put it down to stress. Then there were the down days. I'd just feel this intense sense of sorrow inside of me. It started off as every now and then, but was increasing in frequency. I'd been to counselling, which just seemed to reinforce that there was something wrong with me. You've got this life and you're not happy?

Not long after that, I clocked up ten years with the same company and was given two months extra paid leave. Buoyed by this and assured that I had a job when I returned, I decided it was time to take the trip. I was excited. I immediately booked an around the world ticket for myself and my girlfriend. Six months in South America, three months in Europe and three months in Asia was our rough plan.

The trip was just incredible. It was different from how I usually travelled. Instead of running around and ticking things off the major tourist sites, we took it slow, doing exactly as we chose in the moment.

With a month left to go of my leave, I knew I had to speak to my manager about returning to work. This year was just supposed to be time out from my career, but as the year progressed, something changed.

So, as I waited for him to call, I began to reflect on my time off. I had lived this time of my life differently. I had done what I wanted to do when I wanted to do it without talking myself out of it.

Then the phone rang. I felt a twinge of pain in my chest as I answered it. The long hours I'd put into building my career and all the hard work were weighing on my mind, but I knew that something needed to change for my well-being. I decided I wanted to continue living life as I had for the last year – free flowing, making choices about what I wanted rather than trying to fit in. I wanted to live life on my terms.

I knew what I had to do.

That day, I resigned from my job from the front passenger seat of our camper van just north of Coffs Harbour. What started as a year off work to travel ended up completely changing my life. I discovered what was missing: the power to choose what I wanted. Today the chest pain and the down days of before are gone and I am doing what I love.

Nick Condon

56

Happily Ever After and Divorced

My world came crashing down around me. How did I get here? There I was, sitting on my bed, my sister talking to me. Words were muffled, and my husband was standing by the bedroom door, looking on with a smirk on his face. I wasn't me, I was no longer recognisable. In absolute misery, all that I knew was spiralling out of control. I felt like a child huddled up against a wall of blame.

It felt as if I was being crucified. Was it a bad dream? Was I really in the position of losing everything I'd ever known and loved? 'Hush', the inner voice silenced my thoughts. I was numb, yet at peace. Then the voice whispered, 'Hush, go through this, the answers will come, and you will rise above this. Trust and leave the rest to me.'

I lacked hope and was overwhelmed. How can the love of my life, of 24 years, not be in love with me and want a divorce? I felt depleted. Emotionally, I was torn, heartbroken and in unbearable pain. It hurt like hell. Can you actually die from a broken heart? It consumed me day and night. I didn't think I would ever be able to open my heart to love, not even love for myself.

Physically, I lost eight kilos. I was a shadow of myself. I didn't like what I saw in the mirror. Mentally, it was incredibly challenging to move forward; to keep up with daily tasks, look after my family, work, process all the changes, and handle finances. I needed to regain my independence, power, and strength. Spiritually, my fire for existence was gone. All that remained was a mere spark, a lack of balance and joy in life.

Post-traumatic stress had taken its toll. As much as I had the amazing support and love of my family and friends, my inability to move forward was crippling. I had two beautiful children that needed me more than ever. My turning point came when I knew deep down within my core, I had to change. I was sobbing uncontrollably and went over to a photo of my late father and fell to my knees, calling out, 'Dad, please help me. Give me the answers, show me the way and what I know to be true, the gut intuition of why. Let it come to surface.'

I then no longer allowed my circumstances to bring me down. I finally let go and surrendered. Creating a new life was really important. I commenced each day with beautiful sunlight and fresh air in my home. Morning walks assisted with focus and clarity. One step at a time, my healing process was beginning.

I allowed myself the time and patience to attain personal transformation. The pieces to the puzzle were coming together. It all started to make sense even when it was unpleasant to go through. I learnt a lot about myself. I had dealt with betrayal, loss, abandonment, grief, anger, uncertainty, financial insecurity; I experienced it all.

I began to complete courses of interest, reading self-help books, attending workshops and anything that would stimulate my mind.

With the assistance of natural alternatives, I was putting on weight, looking healthier, and feeling more confident. I chose to improve all areas of my life, using all available resources that I felt were required in assisting my healing process.

I detached from my past by forgiving myself and my ex-husband, moving forward, and embracing the new. Adversity was my blessing and lesson for growth.

I am empowered, independent, and divorced.

Franca Mazzarella

57

Against the Cultural Grain

J arrived in Perth on the 29th of August 2015 to assist my daughter-in-law. Two weeks later, I received a phone call from home. My husband had suffered another stroke. Suddenly my life came to a crossroad. Do I go home or stay in Australia? After speaking to my brother-in-law, I decided to stay, as the social safety net in Zambia would support my husband.

Then my son phoned telling me his condition had worsened and I must fly home. During the flight, I was worried about what would I find as I felt people had been keeping the truth from me.

After arriving in Zambia, stories and accusations flowed. Relatives and doctors accused me of not caring for my sick husband, making his condition worse by unnecessarily taking him to the hospital. Relatives gave my husband African medicines which possibly led to renal failure. My husband was unable to tell anyone. During one visit, a doctor told me that my husband was not a case for the hospital; this was a case for home care. No matter what I did or didn't do, I was criticised. In African culture all the relatives want to have a say in what is happening. So my relationship with my husband's relatives became strained.

People I thought were close to me suddenly turned against me and became my enemies. A girl I had brought up under my own roof tormented me. I was told that each time I took my husband for review at the hospital, I must go with my husband's brother. I wanted to take my husband to South Africa for rehabilitation, but the family told me I could not take him far away from his family. To me, my family was my husband, myself and our children, so it was none of their business.

I employed and paid qualified nurses to help me nurse my husband as it was not only traumatic but emotionally draining for me.

Emotionally, I became irritable. I harboured anger and lost concentration, which affected my work and my health. I lost my esteem. Physically, I started showing symptoms of ill health. Medical tests including a CT scan all were negative. Sleep became difficult. I found myself taking solace in food and this made me put on a lot of weight. My blood pressure and blood sugar also went up.

One day, driving to work, I hit someone's vehicle. I was so absent minded that I only heard a bang. That kind of jolted me back to reality.

I realised I must take control of the situation. As there were no counselling services in our country for me to go to, I decided to consult a colleague of mine, a doctor. I asked her if she could give me something to calm my nerves. She refused. She said, "Anne, forget about those people, because that's their perceptions of you and you cannot change it. I can prescribe you some medicine, but once the medicine wears out you will go back to the same situation. Find a way to deal with it."

I kept on telling myself that I must forget and move on. But it was not easy. I knew that if I continued living with the pressure, it was going to kill me. At that moment I just felt I must stand up and fight, and I did just that. One day I passed through a shopping mall. While there, a young lady handed me a flyer about meditation. I read it and went to the meditation the following day. The method of letting go during the meditation brought life back into me.

Now I am enjoying good health. I can now talk about my situation without pain.

Anne Namakando Phiri

58

A Lighter Touch

My story, thus far, has unfolded in three distinct phases, over the course of which my understanding of what 'healing' means has completely changed.

First, after almost ten years of chronic depression, in 1990 I had an experience of 'awakening', or expanded consciousness. This involved a sudden shift into a near-continuous bliss state that lasted several months and was characterized by an unprecedented clarity of mind and a profound awareness of the interconnectedness of everything.

The first 'healing', then, was holistic and while it did include the sudden and total remission of what had been an extremely visible physical symptom - a frightening and acute skin condition on my face that had developed a few months earlier - for me it was the *inner* shift that was primary, as it went straight to the root of what had caused all the unwanted symptoms, emotional and physical, in the first place. Everything was energy and when the whole system was 'vibrating' at a very high level - experienced as bliss - not only were these new doors of perception open to me but a physical symptom such as my skin problem was simply no longer unable to persist.

Seeing this turned my world inside out. Then, in 2005, it happened again, on an even grander scale. This time, there was no dramatic physical healing that others could observe: it was much more exciting than that! Instead, the body and its attendant personalities were — literally overnight - completely transcended as my points of reference. I was transported into a new dimension of consciousness and experienced the pure light essence of self which is the truth of our being.

As the story of body and personality upon which my depression had depended collapsed, an unstoppable wave of creativity rolled in and I began writing a book. This was the spontaneous emergence of my identity as a 'writer' and demonstrates that healing is not just about the body but all aspects of ourselves and our lives.

Ten years later, another transformational wave arrived, changing my outlook once again and giving me the tools to access this power in a much more deliberate way than before.

As beings of energy, not simply small body-bound creatures, it turned out that our power lay not in force but in effortlessness. Seeing this, I stopped trying to 'heal' or 'fix' things: instead, using a softer focus and a lighter touch I simply began to allow my natural wellbeing to re-establish itself.

Emotions were the key and so, making it my top priority to feel as good as I could feel in any moment, I began to 'raise my vibration' using a range of strategies depending on my mood. The improvement was incremental - and so effortless, sometimes it seemed as though nothing was happening at all. Despite appearances, however, I realized that I was shifting the energy exponentially faster than before.

Because the process was cumulative, over time a momentum was created that led to smaller - though still exciting - versions of the quantum-style shifts that had previously seemed to come out of the blue. This was a new paradigm of self-empowerment, opening the door for everyone to consciously access their own infinite power to heal.

Hilary Cave

59

Healing to Freedom and Fullness in Life

*A*t primary school, I was a sensitive boy. I deeply felt all emotions: happiness, sadness, fear, hurt, and anger. I was allowed to express most of them at home, except anger. My mother was the nurturer of my emotions and my father was absent from my emotional life. I was good at tennis, soccer, cricket, hockey, drawing, painting, and dancing. I would win competitions at school.

The day I started high school, something changed in me. I huddled with some of my friends from primary school and I said to myself, 'I need to harden up if I am going to survive.' So I did just that. I put on a mask.

I would withdraw on the inside and put on a tough exterior. This brought up much anxiety and I became disconnected from my true self. By the age of 16, I was very depressed and repressed to the point of suicide. I thought there was something wrong with me as I had lost the ability to express myself.

I carried this armour all the way through my first marriage until the marriage ended when I was 33 years old. I was then faced with the dilemma of determining 'who I am'. My identity was based on my job as a successful electrician and having a 'successful marriage'. This was to the detriment of my own health and wellbeing. I burnt myself out by pleasing others. Emotionally, I was shut down.

I started the journey to 'reclaim myself', to reclaim my childhood innocence as a man. Dropping my armour was going to make me extremely vulnerable and it took great courage. I have found that most healing and growth have occurred in and after significant intimate love relationships. I have had three marriages, and I value all my healing, growth and learning from those relationships.

But the most significant healing moment happened at a six-day silent retreat named 'Healing Life's Hurts'. This was an amazingly painful and freeing grief journey with my divine true self (my God or my BIG LOVE) and myself as a hurt boy.

Sometimes I wonder, 'Did this journey have to be so long? Did I have to go through all this pain and suffering?' For me, the clear answer is, 'Yes', it all happened for a reason. I learnt to feel again that being in a male body has all been worth it. I can now feel my body, instead of being numb to it; I can feel and express my emotions without fear or shame. I can work intuitively with myself and others and allow BIG LOVE to guide me. I feel so much more alive in my body.

The greatest healing for me was overcoming the social and cultural conditioning of what I believed it was to be a man. Learning it was okay to feel the fear, pain and shame that had such a strong embedded hold on me, because I believed if I showed these emotions, I would not be a man.

My calling now in life is to support and help others heal and grow from the cultural trauma of gender issues, especially men. I also work with couples to heal the cultural conditioning within their relationship and help them connect on a deeper level for a more fulfilling intimate love relationship.

My current partner and I experience a deep and fulfilling relationship because we understand we are together to heal and grow. This is the ultimate connection that many do not achieve in their lifetime.

Robert J Grimes

60

Fiercely Determined

*I*n December 2014, a friend and I left our husbands at home and headed off to Melbourne for the weekend to see our 80s heartthrob – Rick Astley (no judgement, please!). The weekend was filled with eating out, drinking, and enjoying the dulcet tones of our idol.

On that Saturday morning I woke up with a 'pins and needles' sensation running from my waist down to my feet and in both my hands. I had no idea what was going on, but I knew it was serious. I remember going out to breakfast and calling my husband, Marty, and explaining the feeling in my body and said, 'It's not right, this isn't good.'

After I flew home, I went to the hospital, saw my GP and was sent for MRI tests. I was then quickly referred to a neurologist. I sat opposite him as he gave me the MRI report to read. I don't remember reading it properly as words I had never seen before popped out of the page: demyelination, C3-4 lesions, etc. I turned the page over and saw the words 'multiple sclerosis'. I felt myself take a sharp intake of breath and my eyes filled with tears. I looked up at the neurologist and he asked me, "How do you feel about it?" And I replied, "I've had a shitty day at work, and I thought I'd be more prepared for this. Now, what are we going to do about it?"

I spent Christmas Eve in hospital and then four more days of treatment to try and ease the attack on my spinal cord. I immediately began researching MS in more detail to understand the disease and what else I could do to stay on top of my symptoms and manage the progression.

I decided very early on in my diagnosis that MS was not going to define me, nor would it stop me pursuing and doing the things I loved. In fact, it was the giant kick up the bum I needed to make some significant lifestyle changes. And, if anything, it made me even more determined to follow my passions, find my purpose, and succeed.

I decided to take a holistic approach to my well-being. The first thing I chose to do was set myself a fitness goal. Exercise had not been on my radar for some time, so I decided I would train to run the 12k City to Surf and raise money for the MS Society at the same time. I have completed the 12k run each year since, and recently completed my first half marathon!

Next, I had to overhaul my diet. And I mean overhaul! This was a challenge for me (probably more so than dealing with the MS). I also invested in nourishing my mind. I am a self-confessed nerd who loves to read and loves to learn and so I delved into various studies and read many books.

It has been so important for me to surround myself with people who 'get it'; people who know that just because I have this medical condition, know that I am still the same person. I still crack jokes (often about myself), I still moonwalk around the office, and I still eat chocolate – I just happen to have green smoothies for breakfast now instead.

I am grateful that I was diagnosed quickly as it enabled me to implement some much-needed changes in my life. And because of this I actually feel better than I did. I have more energy than ever, and I am fiercely determined. I made a choice about my diagnosis: it was going to be the best thing that ever happened to me.

Hayley Scott

61

Confessions of a Personal Trainer

"C'mon! Five more! You can do it! I know it hurts! Pain is just weakness leaving the body!" As I was encouraging my client in the gym, secretly I was wondering why she wasn't losing weight. After all, she trained with me three times a week, went for a run every day, and said she eats healthy. And she kept telling me how important this was to her. I'm not proud to say it: I used to judge overweight people. Lots of us do, we're conditioned by our society to do it from a very young age.

I grew up thinking that only lazy people couldn't lose weight. It was an easy assumption to make for someone who was naturally fit, sporty, and lean. Also, conventional wisdom tells us: if you want to lose weight, eat less and exercise more. So how come so many of my clients couldn't lose weight and those who did very quickly gained it all back?

I set out to find answers.

I got them in a form I could've never imagined: I started putting on weight! BOOM! Just like that – my six-pack disappeared almost overnight. Luckily, I knew what to do: exercise more and eat less.

And that's when my world fell apart. No matter how many hours a day I spent in the gym and no matter how much I dieted, the weight didn't budge. If anything, I was putting on more and more. Shock! Horror! My own strategies stopped working for me.

I decided to study nutrition to find out the 'perfect diet' for me. That helped a bit, learning which foods were best for my body. But all the knowledge didn't help when it came down to sticking to my meal plans. Being 'good' for a few days usually caused a massive binge in evenings and on weekends. Bloated and disappointed the following morning, I'd promise myself that I'd never do that again, only to repeat the same pattern a few days later. I started to understand the phrase 'vicious circle'.

And if you remember that judging I told you about at the beginning, it all turned against me now. That negative voice in my head, oh boy, the nasty things it said about me! Barking insults for my inability to fit the previous image of myself. I had never been a confident person and now I had hit rock bottom. For a while, my life was a mess; during the day, I pretended to be a successful personal trainer and karate coach. As soon as I was alone, the self-hate and anxiety ruled my life. My family life suffered and my business plummeted, as I wasn't able to make decisions. Fear of making mistakes and being found as a fraud paralysed me.

There was one thing that saved my sanity – curiosity. By this time I knew there must be more to losing weight than just exercise and diet. As I kept searching for answers, I was very lucky to meet incredible mentors and coaches. I learnt what was happening and how I could change it. I started to pay attention to my thoughts and feelings and decided to choose only the best ones for me. I used affirmations, self-care, forgiveness, and gratitude to learn how to love and accept my body the way it was. The weight started to melt away slowly and without much effort. And the best part was, when I stopped judging myself, I stopped judging others as well.

Now I truly believe that I needed to go through this lesson to learn compassion for others. What seemed to be a disaster when it happened to me was truly a blessing in disguise.

Slava Komzic

62

Hope on Hold

*I*t's a strange thing when circumstance hits you in the face and leaves you numb with nothing but the remnants of your life scattered, bloodied and bruised. At sixteen my life took a 'king hit'; I became an instant quadriplegic while playing schoolboy rugby. Despite the unforgiving judgment of a broken neck, the reality of it all was anything but instant.

My story starts in a bed within the spinal unit where doctors diagnosed my injury, "We don't know if you will walk or if you'll get back any movement at all. We will only know more in time." The uncertainty was paralyzing. When a person injures their spine, they experience something called 'spinal shock.' Nothing worked below the break; no feeling, no movement nor other things like temperature control, bowel or bladder. It's like tuning a television, and all you get through your nervous system is white noise. The horrible exception was blinding neuropathic pain whenever I was touched.

The picture wasn't quite so rosy as all that. To stabilize my neck, my head needed to be drilled and calipered with a 5kg weight. Limited breathing caused bouts of phlegm to build-up enough that could drown you in minutes. Bed mirrors were setup so I could see more than the ceiling. Surgical dressers perform the gruesome but necessary bowel and bladder evacuations. Despite the dark times, unconditional hope was born by the caring faces of those that surrounded me.

Each day there was a ritual that doctors would perform; they'd line up at the end of the bed and read through the latest notes. Then with solemn purpose, as much as any priest, would prick the soles of my feet with pins to see if there was any feeling or function. The ritual, in my mind, became a sacrament of hope.

Months went by as my spine slowly settled without feeling or function, so I became a convert. Hope was not lost but held with both functionless hands. Life does that to you, when circumstance throws a roadblock; you grab what little hope there is and hold on tight. Despite the doctors of medicine, who preached hope based on science with their battle cry, "you will know in time", reality rules the battlefield. In two years, the spine stops trying to reconnect. My body's healing had a deadline.

I spent five months in hospital, then a year in rehab. All the while, I sought my own form of absolution. I listened to my parent's tough love, "You'll have it harder than most, but you'll survive. We'll support you against the problems that your disability causes, but you have to do the rest." My parents expected me to do no less than the brilliant success attained by my brothers and sisters; go back to school and finish the HSC, then university, work and marriage. My life revolved around living by my parent's creed and solving the ever-present logistical issues of surviving with limited mobility.

I remember the two-year anniversary of my injury, 'the deadline'. I realized that those years of hoping to regain hand or leg function were only a temporary tonic to the immediate peril of the unknown. My focus had shifted to problem solving the minutiae of life that builds and compounds to better one's life. How true the adage, 'Take care of the pennies and the pounds will take care of themselves.'

Now, I am a man 51 years young; I'm a brother, husband, friend, neighbor, IT analyst, employer, and author. I've rationalized the hope on hold. I've more than survived, I've thrived.

Tony Brown

63

Conscious Love and Hormones

*J*n 2016, I was given a word to chant by a trusted mentor. I was very excited knowing that sound is a tool to regulate ourselves. To my surprise, the word had to do with understanding greed, jealousy, lust, vanity, and attachment. I was insulted and hurt. I wondered, 'Are you saying I am all of these things?' I wanted a word that would develop more peace and love. But nevertheless, I sang this word faithfully.

After eight months, I noticed that I was feeling jealous. If too many girls were talking to my husband, I would feel a twinge of jealousy. It came up time and time again for another two months. I was prescribed some flower essences, went to an Aboriginal sweat lodge, and yet the feelings of jealousy were getting stronger.

Then, just like that, my health exploded. I got a severe rash all over my body; I started getting hot flashes, I was very irritable, my heart was racing, I was exhausted. Visits, to three different doctors and tests showed I had hypothyroidism and absolutely no progesterone. I was menopausal at 38 years old?! What? No! I wanted to have another child!

My heart sank. How could this have happened? After all the families I have helped, you are telling me that I have the same challenges now? I was embarrassed and angry. God, please help me!

I often used prayer to ask for more guidance in how I could serve those who came to me. Perhaps this time my prayers would be answered through my own personal journey. So, I was on a mission. I took a single herb, did acupuncture, used prayer, and had incredible HeartMath sessions.

One day, the last patient of the day came to see me for care. She was telling me a story about a coworker and the tone of her voice was off. Then it clicked, she was jealous. I mentioned this to her, she said, "No," and kept talking. All of a sudden, the room started to expand, time stood still, and her voice got faint. It was like a scene out of a movie. It hit me, Oh no, I AM jealous. The word started to take shape and almost had a life of its own. I realised that many times when I was excited by a new project, felt determined, enjoyed success, invited others to cool events, wanted to show my husband I could provide too; all of these were actually driven by JEALOUSY and not the heart, and it was harming me. This realisation changed everything.

That was the last day that I had a hot flash. My rash cleared up the following week, and I went back to the doctors six weeks after my initial blood work. My thyroid and progesterone were in the normal range. They were shocked. What had I done?

In a word, I had faith; I was willing to stay aware. I sought out help from all areas of care, I was patient and persistent. I had to face my own imperfections, and I had to connect to my heart truly. It took a moment for it to all come together.

In the months after, I have gained more understanding about greed, lust, vanity and attachment. These words have become dear friends of mine that keep me in check when I move further away from my heart and have helped me immensely in my practice.

I love you, Sabrina. I am sorry I taught you that your value lay in always being the best. Please forgive me for not paying attention to what you truly needed. Thank you for being so persistent and bringing me back to my heart.

Sabrina Souto

64

Healing Hashimoto's Through Awareness

*A*fter four years of intense stress at home and work, my memory began failing, my concentration declined, and I had back, hip and neck pain, sore arms, itchy skin and restricted mobility. I was supporting my partner and his child, working full time, juggling work overload and change, all while trying to create a connected family.

The voices in my head were stuck in a loop, on repeat. I'd become upset, angry, sad and unhappy. I felt overwhelmed, experiencing anxiety and depression with my every thought consumed by my situation. I couldn't enjoy the outdoors, gym, and adventure activities that mattered to me.

I wanted peace, not the raised voices, tension, and drama that came with my partner's separation and custody processes. Feeling exhausted, I wanted sleep and for my racing mind to stop. I'd had enough.

After years of working on high-pressure projects, long hours and my health deterioration, my performance at work had slipped beyond recovery, which added to my stress. Each day, I went in wanting to do my best and left work feeling like I'd failed. I was emotional and in tears, which was unlike me: I was normally in control, focused and driven.

I turned to something I'd always loved, but not given myself permission to prioritise: I studied nutrition and reignited my passion for personal development. My path led me to Dr John Demartini, where I was introduced to concepts that shifted my perception, including the awareness of there being equal benefits and drawbacks in every situation.

I went to a doctor and was diagnosed with Hashimoto's, an autoimmune disease, hypo-thyroiditis and adrenal fatigue. There was a feeling of relief, there was a reason I was losing my mind. Then came the thoughts... How can this be? I 'd always been fit and healthy. What did the diagnosis mean? I left the specialist with more questions than answers.

MY health now became the priority for me; not the health of my stepchild or partner. MY health. The research began. I wanted to know what I could do to help myself. After all, a cut finger heals without me thinking about it. This was more than a cut, so I knew I had to support my body to heal.

Healing must be holistic; we must include the body, mind and soul.

Two and half years after the diagnosis, I was able to see the benefit of my illness. I'd become a priority to me, in my own life. The diagnosis related to the thyroid gland. I learnt that the thyroid represents our voice, communication, holding back, and carrying other's burdens and worries.

I started asking myself: Where was I not speaking my truth? Where was I holding back? I found it: I wasn't speaking my truth to myself about what I wanted for my life. I wasn't living my life aligned to my soul purpose. I'd taken on someone else's problems and issues. With this realization, I noticed a release of pain. I'd been stuck in the stories I was telling myself, and memories of my past hurt kept me suffering.

After being told I would be on medication for life, I'm delighted to be medication free. I'm back enjoying laughter, the sunshine, fresh air and adventures that I love. I've stepped out of the corporate role and I now live the life I choose, supporting women struggling with their health. There is hope, we can heal, our body works at healing each and every day.

Kim Guthrie

65

One August Wednesday

*S*ometimes I like to time-travel. I have no DeLorean, no flux capacitor only Gmail search to show me the emails I sent and received on a particular day. I looked back at Wednesday, August 10th, 2016. I was disappointed. There were invitations to events and unopened newsletters, but nothing important, nothing to signify the magnitude of the day. Why was I looking at that day, particularly?

It was the worst day of my life. That day, in Belfast, Northern Ireland, my family and I were on our summer holiday: a last minute, four-night camping trip to the cheapest campsite we could find. One debt after another had eroded whatever savings we had: I emptied my PayPal account – a princely €200 – for spending money for our four-day getaway from reality, and we hit the road.

On the Wednesday morning, I hopefully inserted my card in the ATM to check my balance: zero. I tried again, hoping the 'Available funds' would magically change.

Expecting that a PayPal transfer would go through overnight was naive. I was, at last, broke. I had feared this day for years. I was totally and completely broke. We went to IKEA. It was summer, and IKEA, the family-friendly lifesavers that they are, were laying on a full day of face painting and storytelling. Our last €10 note covered our lunch bill. I vividly recall writing on that IKEA receipt: 'THIS WILL NEVER HAPPEN AGAIN.'

All my adult life, I had lived in a state of perpetual fear. I was afraid of change, stagnation, failure, and hitting rock bottom. There's only so much fear you can take before it eventually starts eroding your mental equilibrium. Several times, doctors had given me sick-notes for time off jobs I just couldn't face. One said, sternly, "Gastroenteritis."

"Nobody ever questions gastroenteritis," said the doc. I didn't have gastroenteritis. I had depression. I don't really remember a time when I hadn't.

My depression was like a thick grey fog. I could see no way forward, and no way back. I told one counsellor that as I left the train at the end of my commute, I took advantage of the wind whipping off the Liffey to let the tears flow. "Are you crying for what you're going to, or what you're leaving behind?" he asked. My response was 'both, neither and everything.' Wednesday, August 10th, 2016 was my ground zero. When the worst happened, and the world didn't end, everything suddenly seemed a bit more manageable. I spoke to people I trusted. I asked for advice and help honestly, openly, and vulnerably.

I committed to one small thing, one week at a time. Depression didn't kill me. I was lucky; it kills so many. For years, through repeated visits to doctors and psychologists, I resisted calls to medicate. That might treat the symptoms, but I could see no hope if I didn't confront the cause.

Instead, I made some hard choices – better choices. I realised I had been working in an environment where falsehood was not only tolerated, but was encouraged. I quit my job. I realised that a life without honesty is not a life for me. So I started to speak honestly, and found that people recognised and valued it, perhaps because honesty is so rare. I realised that, while choosing to be happy is almost impossible, my everyday choices had a massive impact on my happiness.

I'm not out of the woods yet, I might never be. I still allow the tears to come. But I'm here, and I want to be everywhere, and I'm happy about that.

Shane Breslin

66

Overcoming Depression

*A*t ten years of age, I started to experience anxiety. As I grew into a teenager, the anxiety worsened into depression. To the outside world, my life must have looked amazing. I was a super star at sport, top of my class academically, and I had a loving family. But inside, my world was in turmoil.

Inside, I hated myself. The negative thoughts dominated, with the same stories repeating themselves over and over. I felt trapped in a bubble of excruciating pain. I looked out of the bubble and saw others enjoying life and wondered what was wrong with me. I knew I had a lot to be grateful for, but I just couldn't feel gratitude. I wore my brave face all day and cried myself to sleep every night.

My inner world got so messy and unbearable that I thought about suicide on a regular basis. For three and a half years, I was on medications. It was a band-aid that worked while things were going okay, but there was always an overwhelming amount of anger, hate, and resentment towards myself. On several occasions, I ended up at the emergency department in a panic attack, shaking and begging for help.

One day I came across a movie, *The Secret*. I tried all the manifesting techniques suggested, but nothing changed. I thought that if I had the car, the money and the relationship then I would be happy. Within a day of giving up on the law of attraction, I received an email advertising a talk titled, *Beyond The Secret*, by Dr. John F Demartini.

I had no idea where the email came from. The speech promised to deliver the other insights I needed to make the law of attraction work. I was almost broke, but I boarded a train down to Melbourne to attend the free speech. To my surprise, his words made sense. Not much in my life had made sense up until this point.

Eventually, I got myself to one of his programs. During the day, John shared his understandings about life. At one point, he looked directly at me, and although I had hidden myself in the back row, his words penetrated my soul. 'Depression is only a comparison of your current reality with a fantasy that you have imposed upon your life. Clear the fantasy and you clear the depression.'

That night, I worked through my pain and my fantasies. With help, I broke through my blockages and cleared my shame, guilt, resentment and fear. Finally, I could feel love and gratitude for the people and things I had in my life and for my experiences. I couldn't believe how blessed I really was.

After the experience, I took myself back to my cheap hotel room. The whole world seemed different. It felt safe. I pondered the magnificence of what I had just experienced. As I sat in awe, the words came to me, 'I've got you now.' A sense of peace and calm fell over me, and I knew that I would be okay.

The words continued to pulsate through me for almost an hour, 'I love you and I've got you now.' I had never felt as though I had myself to rely on. This was a very new feeling. I could finally begin living, rather than just surviving. I went off my medication that night with no withdrawal symptoms. And whilst the journey of healing did not end there, I knew there was no going back.

I no longer suffer from anxiety or depression. I have a beautiful husband and daughter. Every day, I feel blessed. I believe the real secret to life is that we are here first and foremost to love and understand ourselves.

Sally Moore

67

Surviving Trauma Through Dance and Relationships

*G*rowing up, my life was one of depression and distress. Words cannot describe the feeling of sadness and helplessness I experienced as a child growing into adulthood. I remember how I was bullied at school as well as my mum's bruised face as a result of abuse from my dad. I can also remember the nights when we were all too scared of Dad coming home, drunk and abusive, with mum trying to hold the family together.

I remember the anxiety attacks too, which brought about hyperventilation when confronted by my ex-mother-in-law. Not to mention the struggle of many years of mental and emotional abuse at work.

My life saviours have been my partner and soulmate Jeff, my family, friends, and my ballroom dancing. I didn't realise just what I was being saved from, until recently. During a recent conversation with a counsellor, I realised I was like so many I have seen on TV, in the papers and so on... the ones who were 'victims'. I was one of them.

I knew I needed to know more. I wanted to grow away from what had been haunting me all my life. Apparently, I was a victim of severe abuse. I had to act or I would just get worse, despite the best intentions of those closest to me. Now I could appreciate who I was behind 'the mask'. I didn't want to go back to those dark days. I didn't want any more depression, sleepless nights or self-destruction.

I had been beating myself up, losing confidence, with no self-worth for too many years. I pretended I was good, but deep down inside I was hurting. Through it all, I always kept a smile on my face. I started to think about my life. I didn't want to leave this Earth without leaving a family legacy – a legacy so different from that which I was handed. I always wanted a perfect family, a partner, children, and grandchildren. I want to be around for a long time for my loved ones.

My life is still evolving, and the memories are still there. I know I must learn from the past and move forward. My love for music and especially dancing are my saviours. I can escape from everything. They guide my moods, and take me to another dimension. When dancing, nothing can hurt me. I draw people into my fantasy world, and they comment with, "How beautiful you dance. You are so mesmerising to watch." This is very different from what I heard for far too long. The feeling I have when dancing is very hard to describe, it is so deep within my heart. It is the best feeling ever.

People are now telling me how good I am. These amazing people, full of kindness and support, have helped me realise I have something deep inside of me I can share with others.

I am strong, confident, and beautiful. I always was...but nobody told me. Now I have my partner, my family, and my real friends. I am whole... or at least well on the way. I have come out the other side so much better equipped to face anyone and anything.

I can and I will.

Maree Malouf

68

Rebirthed

*T*he decision to have a baby felt like a full-bodied YES. I was so ready for this moment. What I wasn't ready for was the deep depression I started to experience the moment my partner and I decided that now was the time. At first, I thought that maybe it was the idea of losing my freedom, but I knew that wasn't it. So, what was it?

The guilt of feeling so depressed when trying to get pregnant was massive. I didn't feel I could talk to anyone about it, as I knew that soon I would probably be announcing a pregnancy. What would people think? Should I not be trying? I decided at that moment to see a psychologist and do some self-development work.

Almost immediately, I realised what was happening. I had become small. I had created a life around me that was extremely safe. Bringing a child into this world seemed like culturally the right thing to do, the right time. But thinking about a child looking up to me, I soon realised that I was being a fraud. I was not living passionately, fully and authentically. Who had I become?

I had always been a creator, performer, traveller, and teacher. But in 2013, I had experienced the loss of many of my creative friends to horrific and traumatic deaths. At the time, I was studying singing at the Melbourne Conservatorium of Music. I spent months unable to leave the house. When I would get to the occasional singing lesson, I couldn't sing without bursting into tears. Singing had become too emotional. The fear part of me decided to take over, get me through my course, and then completely stop singing and go into primary school teaching.

So that's what I did for the next three years. I knew I was missing a big part of who I was, but it was safe. Soon, I started to forget what it felt like to be 'me'. But now that I was trying for a baby, it all came flooding back. The idea of not being true to myself, and maybe one day acting out, or trying to live vicariously through my baby did not sit right with me.

I knew that she would look up to me and if I didn't change things, she would end up putting everyone else first and living in fear of her dreams. I didn't want that. It was time for me to come back.

The birth of my baby was the most powerful day of my life. I not only birthed the most incredible little human who burst my heart open, but I spent the entire labour in awe of the sound I was making. Who was that woman? I had NEVER heard sound like that; so connected, so primal and powerful. That was me. I felt like I birthed my voice back into the world.

The moment I heard my baby cry, I started releasing so much and couldn't believe that I had gotten the birth that I wanted. I realised that I had found my voice. I had sifted through everyone's fear, negativity, birth trauma, the 'what ifs', and trusted in what I primarily knew I could do.

Six weeks later, I was living fully from my heart and signed up for courses that would help me come to meet my true voice and support me in starting my business. Again, the guilt came in, but so did a deep knowing that this was the right time. I opened my business with a four-month-old baby and am now bringing people healing and freedom in their creativity and self-expression.

I am here! I have been rebirthed.

Cat McRad

69

Katina the Peacock Living in the Land of Penguins

J was told by my parents that, to be successful in life, I had to study hard, go to college, get a good job, retire, and then enjoy life. And so that's what I did. I worked for a multinational corporation; I climbed many ladders and managed large teams. Without noticing though, that as a single mum, I was very stressed out emotionally.

As an executive, I moved to different countries every three years, but my heart was filled with guilt for not being a present mum. I also noticed my distinctive identity, I was just like a 'penguin living and working in the land of penguins'. I wore the unique black and white penguin suit. I walked and talked like them, I competed with male 'penguins'.

I felt comfortable being around other 'penguins'. I learnt the 'penguin' stride very well. I desperately wanted not only to be a 'penguin', but the best of them. I attended the company's expensive training programs on how to develop the penguin-like behaviour and soft skills. Soon, I learnt that, in a land where they all look alike, standing out in the crowd is a demanding job.

Something began to change below my black and white suit. Something was growing inside, a force that wanted to expand like wings of feathers trying to break through my penguin suit. I didn't understand the feeling; it was uncomfortable. One day, my boss informed me that my only career option was continuing my gypsy life. At the same time, my boyfriend asked me to come to Australia and live with him in beautiful Noosa. By then, my guilt of not being a present mum was suffocating and unbearable, the force inside my penguin suit was harder to contain, my desire for instant gratification was beyond me. I was a successful penguin in a free fall to severe endometriosis and anxiety.

In Nov 2007, I took my chance: I left my penguin friends, my family, and my possessions behind and moved to the Land of Opportunities. I arrived in Australia with only my daughter and my courage, and that day, I began my most profound soul and personal evolution.

But again, I landed wearing my black and white suit with the pride of a successful penguin. I started noticing that the world was much bigger than the Land of Penguins; out there, successful mums, business people, entrepreneurs, artists, etc. are expressing themselves to their best. Who was I? Without my penguin suit, I was left uncomfortable naked, vulnerable, without direction and with little self-worth.

I wanted to know my identity; and the right people and mentors started crossing my path teaching me how to get in contact with my true self. One day, I finally understood: I am a peacock! And I gave myself permission to own it. My feathers are colourful and magnificent and when I open my wings I allow others to open theirs. I finally understood that the Land of Penguins and the Land of Opportunities are not places, but states of mind. That the more I tried to fit in (becoming a penguin) the more I felt incomplete, and the implication is that I would end up at a distance from myself and from my essence. But when I live an inspiring life, I can freely open my wings and splash colours along my journey.

My name is Katina; I am a peacock who wants to open my colourful feathers freely in this world- and so do you.

Katina Cuba

70

From Desperation to Inspiration

*I*magine yourself in the darkness of night, gripping what the coroner labels a blunt instrument, adrenalin pumping, ready to expunge a life. As judge, jury, and executioner, my one-man court was about to commit the ultimate act of desperation – to end the person I deemed responsible. I felt my life spiralling, out of control.

One divorce already had made me a part-time dad. Knowing this 'second true love' was over too was soul-destroying and humiliating. While visiting her father in England, she 'revisited' her ex. I agonisingly forgave her confessions but demanded her immediate return home. After a year of her counselling and her anti-depressants, she then 'chose' one of our staff. He soon left town, and we began to heal, but ignoring my plea and under her spell, he returned.

I had crossed the world twice for my non-maternal damsel and still loved her madly. I had crossed the globe twice to put the girl I loved on a pedestal, toiling to deliver all she craved: a castle, animals and enough wealth to travel the world. Me – the invincible entrepreneur, running five businesses at once, I'd make it happen. Except her affairs had insidiously eroded my powers as I awaited her return to her senses. She became a cold-hearted alien being; her warm brown eyes became death-like nothingness, so here I stood, a cold-sweating weapon, fuelled by rage at his arrogance and her betrayal, with my act planned in finite detail. Plastic and a shovel awaited this itinerant worker, who would have 'simply left town'. Seconds from a point of no return, I was desperate to take back control.

Suddenly, a surreal sunray shone down on me like a biblical intervention. An ethereal voice, not of an old codger on a cloud, but my own internal voice, spoke from my intrinsic value system, 'This is not you. You can't do this. This is not WHO YOU ARE. You're better than this.' Physically shaking, my paradigm shifted with relief. It wasn't about him, the pawn, nor her, the lost soul; nor even about blame, but about acceptance. As my 'now irrelevant' nemesis slumbered unknowingly, I shunned mutual destruction and walked away, recognising my true identity returning; but another test awaited.

The torturous card on my pillow said she loved me and would return when she 'found herself', but she squirmed back to her ex. Ridiculous as it now seems, suicide fleetingly became a viable option. I wonder why I felt that worthless.

Despite my wretchedness, having two fantastic children demanded pragmatism: What kind of father could do that? What kind of role model? How could I not be there for them; see them create their own families? She had left, true, but I was still here. Maybe I had 'failed', but only if I chose to make that pain my reality instead of just the end of a chapter.

My pain almost led me to darkness. Now my very existence was at stake. I snapped out of my pity party and redefined 'me' with a vengeance, inspired to be a better person. Divorce is no picnic, but hindsight brings elation because it shaped my strength of character and created confidence in my capacity to endure.

Dusting yourself off after you've fallen is when your true test begins. That's when you realise that your life can be whatever you choose. My choices led me to travelling, coaching, writing, and presenting; inspiring hundreds of others in need. My best lies before me. So, choose well by listening to your inner voice – your best friend and spirit, for it sees your true potential and can heal you by changing your darkness into light.

Tony Inman

71

Lessons in Love

"*Y*ou'll never have any friends, and no one will ever like you if you do that," said my mum as she noticed the eraser I'd pinched from school. I really liked that eraser, but I believed her. She was my mum, the authority on my world, and that was it. No one will ever like me... I was cursed and doomed for eternity.

"That's not new!" said the Head Teacher, with a tone of ridicule. I'd gotten it wrong again. This time it was 'Show and Tell' in assembly. I stood up to show the whole school an abacus made with beautifully painted bright multi-coloured wood. A classmate had given it to me, as she'd gotten two. Imagine my humiliation. It was new. In my mind it was new to me, and here I was feeling guilty of deceit, wrong and deception in front of the entire school. I looked up to the Head Mistress and here I was again, ill-fated and feeling small.

Family re-location meant I changed schools mid-year. 'Who taught you to write like that?' I was sitting at a little table in a reception classroom with my new teacher. As the question was asked, five and a half year old me picked up on a sense of disappointment in the teacher's voice. I'd written my name in capital letters and begun on the right side of the page heading towards the left and not vice versa. From what I can remember, I hadn't been asked to write very often at my previous school, and now here I was, the second eldest in the class and the only one unable to write my name properly. Yet again, I felt like a huge failure.

"You'll never get onto reading books like the other children if you don't concentrate," the teaching assistant said to me one afternoon, probably a few weeks later – the tone in her voice led me to feel deeply ashamed. Again, I hadn't been asked to look at books very often at my previous school from what I can recall. Well, I was now full of fear and within a year I'd completed the whole reading scheme ahead of most of my classmates and was made class librarian. I started to relax – perhaps things weren't so bad after all! 'AAAAAAAAAAAAAHHHHHHHHHHHHH!!!'

This was the overwhelming sound of my class peers in response to the Head Teacher pulling a piece of paper from the bin and asking me accusingly why I'd wasted the paper. I'm left handed and was simply trying to be neat and had re-started the task.

That's it. I was a VERY naughty girl, not very bright. Nobody liked me. I felt a raw mixture of loneliness, isolation, cruelty, and injustice. My early beginnings were full of constant low-level stress created by my thoughts around these events. There was no murder, starvation or abuse, and I was fortunate to live in the idyllic leafy glades of Solihull, England. Nevertheless, my health inevitably declined.

Years later, I was in a psychology lecture. This is where my moment of spontaneous healing occurred! There's a saying, 'Give me the child for seven years, and I'll give you the (wo)man.' My realisation was profound, yet simple. What we believe and experience in early childhood is crucial to our well-being, mindset, and physical health. I had overvalued what I was not according to others and undervalued who I was according to me.

I now see how the experiences I remember so vividly as traumatic shaped and served me. My new understanding empowered and inspired me to transform myself and taught me the importance of treating everyone with love, sensitivity, kindness, and compassion.

Jo Trewartha

72

Make Your Choices Right

J dislike the question, 'What is your favourite childhood memory?' I don't remember much of my childhood, but what I do remember in clear detail is the trauma I experienced. I know my mum was beaten while I was in the womb; that was where my story begins.

Throughout my childhood, I experienced verbal, physical, emotional, and sexual abuse as well as neglect. When I attempted to run, I was chased, tortured and locked up. Different people abused me without knowing other people also abused me. This trauma was mostly unknown to anyone, my world evolved around survival. I was comfortable in anger, using this to block people out.

My mum left my father when I was 7. I was living with both of my parents week on week off until I was 9, then I permanently lived with mum. I continued to visit my father until I turned 11. Mum filled my life with love and learning, which began my journey of self-healing. At school, I isolated myself, not speaking even to answer questions in class.

When a teacher called my name, I would freeze in shock. Mostly I would answer wrong or not at all, which made both the teachers and students ridicule and degrade me. I can't count how many times I was called 'stupid'. I avoided connecting with others, fearing my trust would be again broken, leaving me to fight my way out.

My teenage years were extremely difficult at first; I created an impeccable mental defence. Attending a workshop, it became clear to me that I was a unique individual and had a lot to give to the world but I needed to do my own healing first. I attended a lot of self-growth and development courses, and cut contact with my father.

I was diagnosed with high functioning autism when I was 14. My mum had taught me what emotions were and how to communicate since I was little. As I began to develop who I was and what I was here to do, I started to stand up to any wrongdoing. I was suspended a lot for calling out and challenging bullies and teachers who abused their power. During these years, I learnt to socialise and make friends, which helped me open up to people and trust again.

I learnt that everyone's experiences shape the way they make their choices, opening me up to understanding that, while I experienced trauma, this was not because of me as a person. Any traumatic experiences these people had are being projected into trauma towards me; this is not my burden to carry. I'm responsible for my choices and future.

I now distinguish my feelings clearly and articulate my thoughts and feelings openly. I understand and connect to others' feelings and thoughts; allowing me to be on their level and work with them through their struggles, side-by-side. Since my healing, I have learnt that my fuel to happiness is love; I now love with all I can, and share this everywhere I am.

I have a lot more to learn and give to others, to aid their healing and to support them in their lives. I know now that we are all different and we cannot change another person's thoughts or actions; however, we can change how we think and act from what we experience.

Even our darkest and scariest experiences can turn our world around as we learn, grow, and change our lives into positivity and love.

Carlosifus Holden

73

Finding Me Within

"Who are you? Where are you? I know you are in there somewhere. Please come back." These are words I would say to myself day after day, month after month, as I stared into a mirror. I had no idea who I was or where I had gone. All that was looking back at me was an image of what I looked like physically. I had no personality, no emotions, no life or light in my eyes. I was an empty shell; a physical body but no one was home.

In October 1977, my car was rear-ended, which sent me into the stationary car in front, giving me whiplash. I was too busy at work to take time off and relied on pain meds to get me through the days/ months/year. Three months after my accident, my husband had his car accident, which resulted in a broken leg and his inability to work for six months. Life became an even bigger challenge now that we were both in pain and debilitated, even the smallest of tasks like making a cup of tea created a debate.

In August 1998, I finally gave in; I could no longer function and was diagnosed with depression. My body had simply shut down, as I had not taken the time for myself to heal. I no longer laughed, I became dull and boring, I rarely spoke; all I could do was nod or shake my head. Afraid of losing my friends, I asked them to 'Please be patient with me, I am in here somewhere, I don't know where, and one day I will be back.' It was a very surreal experience; I was feeling so disconnected, switched off and unable to function.

The first four months of being off work I hibernated, I literally slept all day long. During the next 12 months, I spent many hours looking into a mirror and staring deeply into my eyes and asking, 'Where are you? I know you are in there somewhere. Please come back.' I had no idea how to bring myself back, or how to reconnect myself. I wondered if I would ever find myself again.

Something somewhere was still missing; but how do I find it when I do not even know what it is I am looking for? One day, as I looked into the mirror, I felt myself switch places with my reflection. It was terrifying. It was me who was looking at me, however, I could not distinguish between the reflection and the real person. I panicked. If that was me over there, who was this standing here? As I asked, 'Who am I?' I felt my hand land on my heart; I heard the sound it made as it hit my chest. 'THIS IS ME', I claimed. I then held on tightly with both hands, 'THIS IS ME'. I could feel my heart pounding. I could feel my body vibrating and shaking. I now knew I was alive again, I was back, no longer lost or in limbo.

This was the moment my soul connected back to my physical body. We were reunited and I became whole and alive again – Hazel returned. I began to venture outside the house, which meant I had to get dressed and be prepared to talk to other people again. I began to have mind chatter, conversations where there was once only silence. I began to have desires and plans for the future. Years later, I had friends and my family members describe me in five words; I wrote all those words in a spiral on a round mirror so that whenever I looked in the mirror, I would be reminded of who I AM, and never go down the rabbit hole again.

Today I know who I AM – ME – and I AM PRESENT.

Hazel Butterworth

74

My Healing is Their Healing

*M*y best friend, my two cherubs, and I had boarded the plane in Melbourne bound for Marina Del Rey, Los Angeles. The four of us were all excited about the trip. I had just separated from their father and we had hired an apartment for a couple of months. This was the start to a new life with my children.

Going through LA airport, I saw my friend enter the US while we were taken into a backroom by airport security. I would not see her for six months. Within 24 hours, my children and I were abruptly returned home.

It was a harrowing experience. I was frisked; my bags rummaged through like a criminal while my two children sat outside wondering where mummy was. They were eight and ten years old and had no idea why mummy was being treated this way. Clearly the universe wanted me to return to Melbourne.

We spent nearly 14 hours in limbo not knowing if we were going through or not. I made many prayers to the universe to just let us through, thinking that this all must be a big mistake. The kids were confused but I tried to make it into a game until they put us in the back of a divvy van to drive us to the 'holding rooms'. One tear dropped but I sucked it up not wanting my kids to see.

As they ran around playing games with another detained child, I sat and asked the universe, 'WHY?' Then, as I realised I clearly had further work to do back in Australia, I let a sigh out and just totally surrendered to what was in store for me.

Over the next two years, the universe gave me the answers to my questions. One of the pivotal points in my life was what I thought was an amicable breakup after 17 years.

I learnt about strength deep inside me, which I could have only discovered this way. I learnt that I could stand up to people who threatened me and my livelihood. I learnt to stop giving in to people just to make them go away and give me peace – for in reality that would never stop unless I said, 'No more'.

I am more present with my amazing children. I became the mother I wanted myself – someone who stood up for me, protected me. My children questioned some of my choices at the time, but now they know why. They intuitively knew that I always had their back.

I learnt the meaning of asking for support because I have always been fiercely independent. As a single mother supporting her children, I surrounded them with my family and close friends. They learnt the value of unconditional love as I did. They learnt not to stop being who they are and never just be the norm.

I learnt the value of real love. I left my relationship where I had to walk on eggshells; one of expectations or where nothing you do will ever be enough. When you truly LOVE yourself, you don't search for it in material things and it is not based on conditions, spoken or unspoken.

For me, the day I was sent back to Australia was the day I stepped up to claim back my own power. A mother's love is stronger than the biggest tornado – it can be wild and is a force to be reckoned with; it is also spectacular and magnificent.

Transformation can happen at the strangest and most unexpected moments. Surrendering is never weak; it is simply the strongest thing one can do in certain situations.

Luanne Mareen

75

Healing Through the Heart

*L*ife dealt the cards – whether I play to win or to lose – was my choice. I was at the lowest point in my life, lost, and powerless. I felt like the world and even God was against me. I didn't know what to do or whom to turn to. Yet, one thing I knew was that I was not prepared to give in. I wasn't going to quit life no matter how hard it would be.

One day my heart just opened up – I went to the mirror, looked straight into my eyes and uttered, 'Angela, do you want to be a victim in life and let other people control you, or do you want to do what it takes to live the life you are meant to live?'

I saw two options: the first was to wallow in self-pity, be a victim, let other people use and abuse me, and let past hurt control my life. It was easier to blame others and resent them for where I was at in life. It was comfortable to be in the same place and not change.

The second choice was not easy. It would take a lot of effort and time. I could choose to feel empowered to follow my dreams and discover what I was passionate about. It was way too difficult to make the changes to my life and let go of the past.

I cried and prayed for God to tell me what I needed to do to get out of this misery. I was struggling, feeling lost and hopeless. Yet, I knew there was a flicker that kept the light burning inside me. I knew I could do anything I wanted to. I felt that my life was already planned, and I was here to help people – I knew I had to work through my heart.

I started to walk daily. I meditated every opportunity I had. I looked deep into my heart and found passion; passion to heal through my heart, and to heal others. My heart was so innocent and so pure. I loved people. I connected to people through my heart. I searched for the 'blueprint' of my life. I wanted to know why I was here. To understand what my purpose was. I realised that I had a calling, to make a difference in people's lives. I was already touching people's lives. I was already healing people. I was on the right track. My life was not a mistake!

It was then I realised that I am the driver of my life. I alone can find the path that I am meant to take. No one else is responsible for my life. No one else can control me or ruin my life. No one else can stop me from what I am here to do. It is my life and I was going to make it the best life.

So, I took the path less travelled.

I left my very well-paid job in Sydney, found a suitable country location, set up a retreat to open my heart to help people the way I wanted. I desired to share my life with people. I searched for ways to touch many people's lives. I wanted to share my experience, knowledge, and skills as a critical care nurse and a spiritual healer, to help people live a better life.

Through challenges and adversities, pain and sadness, I found the courage to rise above. I fulfilled my calling.

'I don't go by the rule book. I lead from the heart, not the head.'
Princess Diana

Angela Peris

76

Kundalini Rising

J yearned for the experience of carrying my husband's child. It felt romantic and laced with the love of my life. It was in my daydreams. During the night, it was a different story. Many nights, I would wake suddenly to the same nightmare. Cold, shaky and in total opposition to my fairytale wishes; I would feel trapped, sick to the stomach and uncommitted to my maternal desires.

It was 1999, and I was keen to have a baby ASAP. Friends were popping up with swelling bellies; even two of my younger brothers had 'little ones' in their lives. As I observed humanity's gift of children, their purpose sadly appeared like unconscious cloning, slavery, and accessories, rarely treasured with tenderness and care by the adults entrusted with their lives. I was going to be different. Pouring unconditional love into my own children I was going to show the world another way. I cherished the thought and struggled to focus on anything else.

Shock treatment put cracks in the model of my one-sided ideals. I no longer knew if being pregnant and having children would bring me only wonderment and joy. These fleeting flashes of midnight madness held me terrified at the thought of being pregnant; I became vulnerable and helpless. What if I couldn't handle it? Nine months could feel like eternity.

What if I could feel baby moving within me and it was painstakingly uncomfortable? What if I was sick and couldn't look after myself, let alone a baby? What if I couldn't afford to stop work and needed to rely on others to care for my child when my will was to be at home smothering them with love? What if the baby wasn't healthy and life ahead was filled with sadness and dread of the next trip to the doctors, or even worse, what if we had to say goodbye too early? Deep fears of heartache and loss came to the surface, but they were nowhere to be found upon rising each day.

Conflicted energies increasingly pushed and pulled at my insides until one morning as I began to dress, the most phenomenal vibration began to form within me. My entire pelvic region shook as an uncontrollable energy swirled fiercely around my highly sensitive base, building momentum as it shot straight up through the core of my being and out the top of my head, in a short, sweet, intense matter of seconds.

I was stunned, with no logical reference. A peace-filled awareness gently washed over me. My lips stayed sealed until six years later when I shared my story with a woman from the local Spiritualist Church. She confirmed my earlier encounter as that of the Kundalini Rising, a term I had not heard before.

I suddenly felt accepting of all uncertainties and my panic attacks disappeared. Two years later and there were still no babies. Confused specialists put me in the 'too hard' basket. My FSH levels were through the roof, where fertility drugs would not have come close. An ultrasound showed four follicles. My faith in divine timing strengthened.

Microsurgery diagnosed and removed one endometriosis-ridden ovary and drained a cyst off the other. Feeling rejuvenated and self-assured I rejected an offer of IVF. After nine months, I made the call to do whatever I could to conceive. Preliminary bloods tests were double-checked to reveal pregnancy hormones and the first of two precious children. Baby number two arrived two and a half years later and without a worry in between from me, as to whether or not I would ever be so blessed.

Natasha Jones

77

Gut Feeling

I was living life according to the worldview: finishing school with good grades, getting a job that paid well, getting married, buying a house, having kids, keeping on the treadmill. To the outside world, I would've looked healthy. I played a lot of sport and was successful; I had my own accounting practice and was happily married with a baby daughter. The perfect life.

I woke up one day in my early 30s feeling sick in the stomach, not able to sleep because of constant reflux and needing to prop myself up in bed. Only through exhaustion would I fall asleep, and I would wake up feeling the same way. After going to the doctor and having every test known to mankind done, they couldn't find anything wrong with me. They thought I was perfectly healthy. This went on for the next 18 months.

As a last resort, I went to hospital and had a camera look around my stomach, which revealed my stomach was full of ulcers. My body was riddled with stress. Awesome! Now that we knew what the problem was, it was time to fix it. The doctor prescribed Somac, which I was happy to take initially, as I didn't want to do any more damage to my stomach. As months passed, I really didn't feel much better. I was still getting reflux, still having difficulty sleeping. The doctor prescribed Losec. More months passed, and I still wasn't getting any better.

It is one thing to know the problem, knowing how to fix it is another. By this stage, I was at rock bottom—I just wanted to feel normal again. I vividly remember one morning resting my head against the wall of the shower thinking there has to be another way.

That morning, I went into work to find someone had slid free tickets to a wealth creation seminar under my office door. I decided to go. For the next three hours, I listened to a successful businessman, who was a millionaire a few times over, explain how to get wealthy. He challenged many of my beliefs. I thought, if half of what he was saying is true, I needed to know. This would be great knowledge to take back to my clients. 'Sign me up,' I said.

My next challenge was explaining to my wife that I had just spent $5,000 and was going away for five days. I'm very grateful she understood as the retreat was amazing and life-changing. Being out of my natural environment opened me up to a whole new world of thinking, giving a new positive outlook on my life and the world in general. I thought to myself, 'Who has been withholding all this information from me? It's definitely not taught in schools.'

I literally threw my medication in the bin as I left the retreat. When I returned home, my wife asked, 'Where on Earth did you go?' It was obvious she could see my newfound energy and enthusiasm for life. We later decided to share the experience together, and to this day, we are very much happily married after 27 years together.

You cannot eliminate all stress and anxiety; I think they are necessary for the full experience of life. However, I now know how to manage these moments while getting a great night's sleep and being ulcer-free.

This experience has taught me that, through our greatest challenges come our greatest gifts; in particular, my self-awareness. To me, how you feel is the most important thing in life. I was trying to please everyone: clients, family and friends. I am 100% responsible for my life and no one else's.'

'What people think of me is none of my business.'

Alan Jackson

78

Being Faye

*T*here was once a time I would cry from the moment my eyes opened in the morning. I was astounded that it was still possible to be breathing, having fallen to sleep feeling so desperately unhappy and displaced. I was on a path of self-sabotage and self-harm. I felt life was without purpose. The fantasy of suicide was fast becoming a reality. This continued into my late teens when I was hospitalised for the third time and diagnosed with bipolar disorder.

During a manic episode, the veil between the physical and non-physical realm began to disappear all together. The fear of what I could sense, see and feel was consuming me. On the one hand, I was aware of what I now know to be a spiritual awakening; whilst on the other, I was in hospital for a diagnosed illness. There was no logical explanation to what I was experiencing, and the confusion between the realities was further blurred by my lack of understanding and a heavy dose of medication. I returned home and moved to the other side of Australia. Here I began the healing journey in my own way.

I sought guidance and was told I needed an exorcism. At this point I was being pulled out of bed by my feet, smothered by my own pillow, scratched and bruised by shadow-like energies that appeared in my bedroom, most often at night when I was alone.

Paralysed in fear, I continued relentlessly consuming drugs and alcohol to avoid being overwhelmed by helplessness and sheer madness that I felt when I was sober. Still unaware that my clairvoyance was active, the paranoia of what I could see, feel, and hear in the non-physical realm tormented me every hour of the day.

My dad witnessed me in one of these attacks. An invisible weight threw itself at me. My dress ripped open and bloody claw marks ran down my back. I wailed in terror, simultaneously feeling relieved, as this was the first time someone else had seen it happen.

This was the turning point; I was in fear of my life and determined to find somebody who could help. The following day, I met with a clairvoyant who changed my life. She gave me clarity and reassurance that I had not lost my mind, and what I was experiencing was real and there was a reason for it. For the first time in my life, I had an explanation that made sense and a knowing that I would find peace.

Under supervision and support of my GP, I gradually stopped taking all medications. I also stopped self-medicating with alcohol and drugs. Huge changes were required in all aspects of my life. I devoted all my energy to healing, and I learnt how to love myself again. Detoxing my spiritual, mental, emotional, and physical bodies, I eventually became clear, strong, protected, and inspired.

Through the process of healing, I gained insight into my own gifts as a clairvoyant. I developed my knowledge through my experience, research, intuition, books, people, and courses that were available. My goal was always to heal myself, and in the process I realised that I had a burning desire to share what I had learnt and utilise my gifts to empower others. It has always been my passion to teach, inspire, and help people to become the best version of themselves, and this journey has skilfully provided the tools for me to do so authentically.

Today, I wake up with my eyes sparkling and a smile on my face. My healing journey bloomed, and carved a path less travelled to health, purpose and peace. And within this journey was a mission to help you find yourself and your purpose here on Earth.

Faye Rushton

79

It's Never too Late for Rebirth

From a very young age, I have been fascinated with 'life' and living things big and small. I was curious and wanted to figure out how stuff works. My parents gave me my first microscope when I was eight years old so I could study dirt, bugs and creepy crawlies that were roaming in the backyard. That simple tool was magical to me; it opened up an intricate world that was beyond the reach of the naked eye. It was a world of wonders beyond that which most people can see or even consider.

For as long as I can remember, all I knew about life was the tangible, physical world, the one you can see, touch, feel, and understand. The obvious one that sits right in front of your eyes and that you learn to make sense of.

This fascination with 'life' and the world of the 'micro' lead me to study biology at school, and then do a PhD in molecular genetics at university. All was fine and good in my scientific career as a medical researcher until about ten years ago, when I suddenly came to realise that there was more to 'life' than meets the eye.

Something unusual happened. One day, out of the blue, I looked at a book my wife, Marcia, had bought. What really caught my eye was the title, *The Universe in a Single Atom*, by the 14th Dalai Lama. As soon as I started to read this book, I couldn't put it down. I ended up reading it from cover to cover in a weekend. I found myself taking a lot of notes, as I usually do, and suddenly found my mind opening up to new possibilities – to a new world that had been there all along but to which I was completely oblivious. Quite frankly, up to that day, the realm of the mind, thoughts, emotions and spirituality were completely foreign to me. These were never really a topic of conversation that came up at home or in my life at all.

That day, a profound transformation took place; something I would never have predicted. A rebirth occurred within me, and my life took a different turn. I started to intensely study and explore spirituality, religion, metaphysics, philosophy, and psychology. I read anything I could put my hands on that was related to human experience and our universe beyond the physical.

It then took me another two years to finally make a decisive step and write my first book. It was something very 'left field' about the mind and body, something I never thought I would do as a scientist. That was the moment I decided to separate myself from the 'classical' scientist etiquette and realise that I was more than what meets the eye.

Intuitively, I realised that my mission and personal journey on this planet was to integrate the mind and body in my studies and work, so I could feel whole for the first time. As a researcher in neuroscience, I was not confined to the purely cellular and molecular aspects of health and disease; however, 'life' had a whole new dimension – a subtle human dimension you can't 'measure' in the traditional way.

That defining day helped me realise how the artificial separation of the mind from the body prevents people from tapping into their full potential. That is exactly why I chose to dedicate the rest of my life to bridge the gap between mind and matter. Integrating my intuition and inner wisdom with my scientific mind, I help people connect the 'dots' of their life and facilitate the changes they need from inside out to unlock their true potential and unravel a clear path forward.

Dr. Olivier Becherel

80

Through the Flame

*E*xperiencing the trauma of separation from my partner, family and community, the pain was deep and unbearable. There was me on this side, and the rest of the world on the other side; I was looking at them through the looking glass.

From this side, I could see others as a 'mirror' of my own pain and suffering. They and I were no different; we were interlinked, yet, I felt so lonely and desperate. It began the onset of so many health problems: agoraphobia, claustrophobia, social phobia, insomnia, depression and chronic fatigue.

I had so much work to do on myself. As Ghandi said, 'Be the change that you wish to see in the world,' which is exactly what I decided to do. As I went deeper and deeper into an abyss of feeling and experience, I knew that if I worked through these things, one day at a time, I would slowly get through. So my motto became, 'One day at a time'. I needed healing on all different levels; here are some of the things I did:

Duvet Days: If I felt I could not get out of bed and face the world, I would hide in my bed and meditate, whilst resting and hibernating, having conversations with God.

By the River: Sitting, reflecting, talking to myself, and gazing at the river, waterfall, and swans.

Music and Dance: At times, I would just disappear into the music and dance, deep into myself!

Tratak (Candle Gazing): The healing part of all this was the daily candle gazing. It was something I used to love doing during our regular *Satsang* sessions as a child; my grandmother would light the *chiraag* every Thursday for our ancestors. It was so comforting and reassuring – such a feeling of warmth and coziness. This is what gave me the knowing that I am spirit, and that all else can be overcome and shall pass.

With the flame, I could be myself. I could communicate and express my deepest feelings of the pain I was experiencing. This was my breakthrough to a journey back to myself, as this technique has been a 'homecoming'. This homecoming was felt one night, though I didn't know at that time what exactly it was, besides an amazing spiritual experience. It is called *Kundalini Awakening*, or entering the light body and receiving 'Darshan'. But what happened on this night was a turning point — I could see my life was never going to be the same.

The flame of the candle played a big part in the act of 'transforming' my life and giving me the guidance that I needed to continue. For me, the flame led me from the darkness to light. This period in my life was the greatest darkness I have ever felt and experienced. There was a loneliness that words here would never be able to describe; however, it has also been my greatest teacher. I had moved from a false self, into my real self.

My journey has been one of 'Life Transformation' Transformation. Healing has occurred in my ability to listen to my intuition and be guided to the courses of action that I took. Now, I am a therapist, tutor, and a help and guide for others with skills that I gained and learnt in my own journey. I now enjoy very good holistic health, a high sense of self-esteem and self-worth. Through the breakdown, I was able to rebuild and restructure my life to a more meaningful way of being.

'The light will be as bright as you want it to be!'

Jaswinder Challi Sahiba

81

You Are Your Own Master!

*J*n July 2012, I attended a personal development workshop, which completely turned my life around when I heard my 'Angels' say at the end of the day, "You are your own Master!" Really? I am my own Master? You're kidding? Right?

Nobody had ever said this to me before. I'd never even heard it said to anyone else for that matter. You see, my life up till then was filled with turbulence and abuse. I'd become a puppet; lots of other people were pulling my strings, and more often than not, I wasn't even aware of this. At times, I'd hint at being my true self only to be beaten to a pulp and I'd become numb – really numb. This often brought about feelings of deep loneliness, despair, and the dire need to check out.

Since I had no one to turn to or trust, I called my 'angels' for support. I'd been working with them since 2003 as an angel medium and found truth, love and safety here.

"You are your own master!"

Initially, change was gradual as I began drifting away from comfort zones I no longer required. By mid-December 2012, another rather strong energetic shift occurred. This took the form of a veil that appeared to me as a horizontal line lifting from the ground up to above my head. Symbolically, it was like raising a window blind to let the light in.

So by early 2013, I started seeing things more clearly and my thinking began to evolve. My attention reverted to my creative self and I began reigniting this long-lost passion into my life even auditioning for *The X Factor* in 2013. Though I didn't get through, I learnt the stage was my home. I saw abusive relationships for what they were and I started letting them go. I even challenged myself around systems designed to control my mind/body when it was deemed I'd have to live with chronic illness – diabetes – for the rest of my life.

I thought, 'I'm taking matters into my own hands. If I stuff up, so be it. I'm okay with that. This is my life, my body, and no one has the right to tell me what to do with it ever again.'

I acknowledged my belief that I could reverse it. After all, what we create, we can 'uncreate'. I did this by participating in a controversial detox program. My blood sugars have been normal ever since. It was also brought into light that I had food intolerances, which contributed to my being unhealthy. I now follow a Paleo lifestyle.

By late 2014, my 'angels' continued, 'You'll do your best work away from here.' So I left the spirituality industry behind. My creativity as an actor, singer, visual artist, writer and business intuitive, is bringing my light into the world in a healthier way.

Finally, it's important to be clear that, prior to the directives from my 'angels' and my change of choices, I'd only ever seen myself as worthless or ugly. But because I'd also incorporated kinesiology and other natural health services, today I realise I've loved myself all along because I did all this for me in spite of my circumstances.

There is truth in 'You are your own master!' The minute I consciously decided to stop putting my life into other people's hands, it became easier to stop listening to all the voices outside of ME. I found myself and though my life is work in progress, I'm now experiencing my life in my own way.

Panayiota

82

The Day I Saved My Life

After nine months of slowly getting more and more tired for no apparent reason, I walked into work one day and quit my dream job. A week later I was diagnosed with chronic fatigue syndrome (CFS) and told there was no known cause or solution.

For three months, I crawled downstairs for the day's highlight: an hour of THE LOVE BOAT. Yes, this was the top priority in my otherwise eventless day. Most friends had no idea what was going on, and even on my worst days would say, 'Gosh, you look so well.' The day the final episode aired, I sat watching the credits roll, and a wave of sadness filled my heart. 'What on earth am I going to do with my days now?'

I felt a stirring in my gut. The sadness transformed into deep anger. 'NO! I will NOT spend the rest of my life unable to leave my house!' In a split second, I made the decision that would change my life, in fact, save my life: 'I WILL find a way to get well! I WILL live!'

The energy that had built up inside of me was powerful. I stomped upstairs. *Bamm bamm bamm*, as my feet hit the steps. It was the most energy I had experienced for months! I had no idea how I was going to get well, but deep down I knew I would, and that I was prepared to do whatever it took to get there. Barely five minutes after that decision, a random thought popped into my head: 'Call Anna'. She told me to buy *Quantum Healing*, by Deepak Chopra, as it would help me see things differently. I was amazed. Here was a completely new perspective I had never heard of before: the mind, body, and energy are connected!

For the next five years, I optimistically trialled and tested 140 natural therapies. Nothing made a dent in the fatigue. One day, bed-bound again, I found myself asking, *'What if I only have six months to live? What if I never get well? What if I die?'*

As I lay there, unable to move, I started thinking about my long-term dream of travelling the world.

'But how can you travel if you can hardly get out of bed?' I thought.

The potential reality of only a few months to live outweighed this practicality, bringing an urgency to take action. *'Wouldn't it be better to die doing something I love, than die bored, lonely, and sick?'* 'OK, let's do it', I heard myself say.

It seems crazy 17 years later that I thought I would die, but at that moment it felt real. It was so real that I made a life-changing decision, which took me on a 14-month journey to seek and finally find the answers.

My adventures found me to a hotel room in San Francisco, barely able to move again. I had travelled to America, the Middle East, Europe, and Central America searching for answers. 'I'd been chanted over in Egyptian sarcophaguses, undergone Guatemalan shamanic healing, sweat lodged in Mexican temezcals, and purified my body in Ayurvedic rituals. And yet here I was, still unable to move.

I made my way to yet another healing session, and the therapist said two sentences which changed my life forever, 'Chronic fatigue is not a lack of energy: it's blocked energy, and specifically blocked emotional energy.' In an instant I understood. A lifetime of emotions poured out of me for the next hour. In the next five years I learned many more 'secrets to health', finally ridding myself of fatigue, anxiety and depression, and then started helping others.

The day decided to live was the day I saved my life.

Kim Knight

83

The Healing Power of Truth

*J*n September 1999, I descended into a hyperventilating breakdown in the middle of a suburban street. I had been struggling with profound sadness and despair, which firmly took hold several weeks earlier when I distinctly recall becoming aware of a physical pain in my chest that felt like my heart was literally breaking.

The following day, I was diagnosed with moderate to severe clinical depression and commenced on antidepressants, which I would go on to take for the next six years. There was some improvement in my overall mood and sleeping patterns, but it was nowhere near enough. During this time, I also consulted counsellors, psychologists, psychiatrists, and even spiritual healers with little, fleeting or no effect. For me generally, life was grey. Sure, it wasn't black anymore and thoughts of suicide had diminished, but life definitely had no colour.

Then one Sunday morning in 2005, my mother called and said she wanted to visit as she had something to tell me. I saw a lot of my mother in those days, but she never visited on a Sunday so I was intrigued. Trying to recapture the correct sequence of events is sketchy now, but my most vivid recollection is standing in the kitchen with mum embracing me and looking into my eyes apologising for not telling me I was adopted at two weeks of age, and therefore not biologically connected to any of the people I had thought I was, all forty four years of my life!

The darkest, deepest chasm appeared in my kitchen floor, and I fell into it. My mother was talking, but I was only hearing the odd word here and there. The rest of the time my ears were filled with a deafening sound not unlike crashing waves. Quite a few members of my family already knew of my adoption. So on top of the shock, grief and feelings of betrayal, came gut-wrenching humiliation.

My heart broke into a million pieces; but at the same time as I was devastated, something inside of me shifted and there was a clear sense of liberation. Finally, a mystery I had been aware of on the deepest level for years was clarified. It was as though I had been handed the final piece of the jigsaw that I would never have been able to complete the puzzle without.

From that point on, I had something to work with in regard to resolving deep emotional pain, finding inner peace and living an authentic life, which were goals I had aspired to my entire life. I stopped taking antidepressants, but as time went on, I became aware of issues I could not shift around trust, rejection, and feelings of abandonment.

In 2016, I found and met my birth mother, which was wonderful and proved to be the catalyst for more profound healing; none of which would have been be possible had I not known 'the truth'. However, her lack of response to any of my attempts to communicate since our meeting plunged me into such darkness and despair that I found myself with little will to live.

Thanks to a life-changing psychospiritual course called *Healing the Core Mother Wounds of Abandonment and Rejection*, I was eventually able to see the entire situation as a gift to help me work through the primal wounds of abandonment and rejection at the deepest level. The secret it seems, for me anyway, is not to avoid feeling negative or unpleasant emotions but to completely embrace them, accept them, feel them, and then breathe them out and let them go. When I find the time, space and courage to do this, I never fail to find profound peace and tranquillity.

Sharyn Bailey

84

Not Seen and Not Heard

I grew up as the fifth child in a family of nine; we lived in a crowded three-bedroom house with both parents working. My parents were very busy and in their own little worlds mostly, not knowing what was happening with us kids. When they argued, I would say to myself that I would never do the same. From a young age I cleaned the house and did the washing. I also cooked if there was food, but at times there wasn't enough to feed us all.

I was on the outside and always seemed to get into trouble. I never spoke because there was no one who wanted to listen or was interested in what I had to say. So I kept my feelings and thoughts to myself, not letting anyone know what I was feeling or thinking.

My school days weren't much fun; I was bullied by the teachers and appeared dumb compared to my brothers and sisters. I felt belittled and insignificant. I left school after grade ten, and was never encouraged to further my education. The teacher said I wouldn't amount to much, which stuck in my mind.

Although I struggled at school and was seen as one of the dumb kids, that never deterred me. Rather, it gave me the strength to be and do things that I never imagined I would be able to.

In everything I did as a young woman, I was determined to do it to the best of my ability. I have always had an attitude of 'I can do anything' and 'never say never'. Now I feel I have the ability, skills, and knowledge to help others to uncover, unlock and unleash their true potential. I think I gained that strength and determination from growing up in such a large family where, if you didn't do for yourself, you missed out; it was all about survival.

My first relationship was abusive almost from the beginning, though I didn't realise it at the time. The abuse continued through our marriage. I saw it as normal. It wasn't until I was doing some study and personal development that I realised that what was going on was not normal. I think I knew it but didn't want to admit it. After learning and understanding that I could change what was not serving me, it still took me a long time to leave the relationship that I had spent 30 years of my life in.

It has taken me a long time to realise that what I have always wanted and expected in my life is beginning to become a reality, especially now that I understand the journey I was on and still am. There have been things I have dreamt about for many years that I have now achieved: becoming a published author, transformational conversationalist, coach, mentor, and radio presenter are just a few things that were on my bucket list.

I now have a voice to create the environment to speak my truth. I am clear about what I want in my life and will push my boundaries if I need to. I never allow the struggles in my life to stop me from doing what I am passionate about.

Today, I am fulfilling my dreams and my passion to be of service, not only to myself and my family, but to those women and children who come from adversity, providing them with a safe environment to be educated and given the ability to go out and live the life they never imagined possible.

My passion in life is to create awareness, educate, and inspire you to be true to you.

Faye Waterman

85

Born Broken

*S*o there I was again, sitting in the pain, heartbreak, and disappointment of yet another broken marriage. I thought he was the one; someone I would grow old with, my best friend and soulmate. I had loved him with everything I had.

I was loyal, honest, loving, caring, nurturing, sexy, spontaneous, and fun, but I still didn't measure up. I looked after his children like I did my own. I'd given up my personal goals, dreams, and aspirations. I even sacrificed time with my friends, family, and myself. I sold the house I had worked so hard to obtain; I neglected my business and totally ignored my own needs and self-care. I gave all of myself in order to be loved, yet I still felt lonely, unloved, and not good enough.

I thought I chose carefully and wisely and had taken the time I needed to clear out the past pains from previous lovers. I had worked on my personal growth deeply and thought I had entered into marriage with a wholesome level of self-worth and tools to create the relationship and family I had always aspired to be a part of. But that was not the case.

I was repeating my pattern of giving all of myself and walking on eggshells to try to make him happy, notice me, show some appreciation, love and attraction towards me. No matter what I did, I couldn't please him – I was broken and full of self-doubt!

How could this be when I had invested so much into my personal transformation and development? I understood the principles to move through life hurdles. I knew how to follow my purpose and achieve great things. I had found resolve and forgiveness towards the hurts from my past lovers, and still the same emotions, beliefs, and circumstances were killing me.

What healed my heart was delving into the subconscious knowing of my conception, the womb, birthing process and early childhood experiences that had unknowingly become a part of all of my relationships. My body's first experiences and memories were with me until I became conscious and aware of them. When I gave healing energy and power to reversing this limiting belief and thought patterns that no longer served me, I was healed and experienced greater joy.

Although I was not conscious of my birth, amazingly, my body remembered it very well. I learnt through my healing that what I had experienced with my mother, father, grandmother, siblings, teachers and other adults from birth had formed my belief system about love, safety, vulnerability, care-taking, power, marriage, communication — everything I needed to feel positive and powerful about in order to have and experience real love.

I couldn't heal until I found awareness, peace, forgiveness, gratitude, self-love, and accountability for the damaging scripts I was playing out in my life. I realised in relationships that it takes two to speak their truth, take responsibility and own their patterns as they arise. Until I became resolved, I kept attracting that which was familiar and recreating the situations that mirrored my childhood heartbreak and pain.

Any pain, fear, judgement, resentment, hate, guilt, or anger not resolved – or anything we may feel we have lost or needed – will come up for healing throughout our lives. My healing was found in removing blame and opening my heart. I found the courage to be willing and able to face my fears; I became accountable for the part I played, forgave others and myself, and surrendered to healing, transformation and truth to now live with wholeness, happiness, gratitude, and love.

Deborah Toussaint

86

Overcoming Depression Without Drugs

*J*n 2010, my wife and I were trying to start a family. The natural process wasn't happening fast enough, so we opted for IVF. It worked and soon my wife was pregnant. This news brought great joy to both of us.

My wife was in Zambia waiting for her visa to join me in Western Australia. On 25th June 2011, while I was in Zambia visiting her, we rushed her to the hospital. It was two days before she was seen by a doctor, but by then baby Lweendo had given up. We were broken beyond words. I left my wife in Zambia the next week and returned to Australia.

I was suffering from depression as we had not been married for long and were living in separate countries. We weren't able to make plans as a family, and we could not do the things that bring brightness and warmth to every young couple's lives. Sometimes, we were so frustrated that we fought, blaming and finding failure in each other.

To add to my depression, my father and mother both passed away from cancer. I returned to Zambia for my mother's funeral but not my father's. I was grieving for my parents and missed Zambia. I even contemplated moving back for spiritual, emotional, and physical support, because I felt empty inside on my own in Australia. But my finances wouldn't allow it to happen.

Because I was brought up in a culture where you did not share your personal issues with a stranger, for fear of being scrutinised and judged, I didn't speak to anyone about my depression. I needed to have trust in the person I confided in. So, rather than speak with someone, I moved on and tried to be strong for myself and my family. I did this by turning to nature to help me heal.

It was the best thing that ever happened to me. Nature cannot gossip, nature cannot look down on you and judge you. Nature brings life and nature is life. It clears the mind and creates that soundness within you.

Sometimes we need to be in-tune with ourselves to nature and pay a little attention to what nature has to whisper.

I found working in the garden, waking up to animal noises, like pigs, birds and chickens, and just hearing the wind blowing through the trees to be soothing. Watching the rain drop on the window played the magic to my healing. Reading a book, writing, and listening to instrumental music also played a part in my healing. Living by the ocean was just amazing; I was just a few metres away from the sand dunes. My bedroom was facing the ocean, and I could hear the water, especially at night when it was silent.

I moved to West Kimberley where I had the privilege of observing the high tides come in and out. I healed just by observing the power of nature in every sense. It is true that sometimes I could not sleep because the visions of our baby boy, my dad, and mother were still strong, but just getting in tune with nature helped me. Sometimes, we do not need to look too far for help.

Today, I feel way better. I am no longer depressed. God is great and we have been blessed with two beautiful children (Chipego and Daniel). When I feel low, I go out and meet people, listen to their stories and have a laugh. That is therapy enough. I am stronger than ever before and, I know how to channel my emotions to better things. There is always something around us if we just pay a little attention.

George Masempela

87

Optimum Thinking Works Wonders

*W*hy can't I just be happy? Why can't I just have the relationship I want? Why can't I just manifest the money I want? Why is trying to be positive not working in my life? Why?

These were the questions I stumbled across when I was about 25 years old. I had come across positive thinking a few years before this and thought I had found the answer to all my questions and prayers. I remember looking up to the sky one day whilst driving, thinking "Great, Manmeet, you have found the answers, all you have to do is think positive!"

A few years passed, and I found in truth, it is this very thought process that nearly got me in to depression thinking my life had no meaning and that it was fate for me to have a miserable life. No matter how hard I tried to think positive and keep smiling, perceived negative things still happened. Inside I was broken and wondering why God had chosen me to give all the negative experiences to. How can there be a God, if he isn't giving me the happiness I want? Is it a better option for me just to exit the planet and end such a life?

In 2008, I sat in a room of 300 people in central London waiting for a man, who I had no idea was about to change my life that night forever – Dr John Demartini. He opened his talk that evening with this one question "Who here is into positive thinking?" I raised my hand up high with the other 299 people in a very proud attitude, still trying to kid myself it was working. "And who here still has negative thoughts?" he went on to ask. Embarrassed of myself, I put my head down but my hand remained high feeling that Dr John Demartini was speaking directly to me. It was then I realised there was no mistake I was there.

That night I was introduced to the concept of Universal Laws that dictate the absolute perfection of the world we live in. I learnt there is never a one-sided magnet in life and both sides are what makes up this beautiful essence of life. All this time I had been striving to seek pleasure, avoid pain, get a positive without a negative. The search for this one-sided life was futile. It was that night, I had a reason to live, and find out more about this way of thinking.

I went on to further educate myself about these natural laws and a few years later I really understood the true wisdom behind them. It was the very concepts I used in order to neutralize past strong, un-resourceful emotional charges. With a scientific background I had a tool kit of quality questions to help me get out of emotional reaction and back in to action by seeing both sides of life and people. It was years later when I met my friend and colleague Helene Kempe, that I truly understood that what I had learned and now practiced was Optimum Thinking!

I no longer wanted happiness alone. I no longer wanted a positive without a negative, I no longer wanted to live a fantasy that was unobtainable! Instead I started to live a fulfilled life embracing both sides of support and challenge. It all just made total sense.

Dancing with this physical existence became possible. Living to my full potential, became possible. Inspiring relationships and health became possible again. But more importantly, it became my life mission to share these tools with others in helping them understand the Grand Organised Design (GOD) and the Divine Perfection in the Universe really does exist and that nobody ever needs to feel like life is not worth living because they are not getting their one sided life – like I once did!

Manmeet Chowdhry

88

Dancing to Different Possibilities

*I*n 2002, I was in a supportive marriage; enjoying a wonderful life. Then the unthinkable happened: my beautiful husband was diagnosed with aggressive lung cancer and passed away three months later. I was devastated. My world came crashing down.

I felt numb, fearful, and overwhelmed. My life unravelled before my eyes. It sapped my energy and life force, leaving me emotionally, physically, and spiritually bankrupt. It was a stark contrast to the vibrant, confident, and energetic person I had been. I pushed myself mercilessly, until my mind shut down and my exhausted body collapsed. I felt that my life would never be happy or fulfilling again.

My weight dropped, I stopped eating. I was intense, driven, and serious, and worked till I dropped. I was in the darkest part of my soul, drowning, floundering in self-pity. I felt hopeless and powerless as old wounds from the past surfaced. I sank lower and lower. I buried and locked away my emotions. I was deep in remorse and lived in anticipation of a pain that tore at my heart and almost paralysed me with fear.

At my lowest point, the doctor asked me a life-changing question, "Don't you matter?" It felt like I had been hit in the face with cold water. The shock flipped something inside me. It was time for action. My mind and body needed serious love, support, and attention. I had hit zero level, rock bottom. Dancing to new possibilities was light years away, but the decision with intention was made. Did I want to live in that sad and depressed state? No way!

I would love to say the universe suddenly handed me a new life in a heartbeat and that I skipped and romped to happiness and joy. However, it was not like that. My scattered thoughts and actions needed reining in, starting with a psychologist whose strategies I use to this day. Writing and self publishing my story of moving on from childhood abuse, a violent alcoholic dad, a gang rape, pregnancy, and abortion allowed me to face and defeat my demons.

I continued to work on my deep emotional issues, and to be more specific, it was a few years before I could get super excited and see a snapshot of my future. My incredible journey of recovery was on its way. I began to focus on how I would survive and thrive. How would I find joy and happiness in my new life?

These words were so powerful; they popped out at me at just the right time. In these words, I found the gentleness I required to support myself: 'If I cradle something ugly in me, I can watch it soften and transform.' As I gained control and power over my life, my confidence and assertiveness returned. I began making better decisions. I checked in, (I still check in with myself) and I saw relaxed aliveness and vibrancy.

As I grew stronger and learnt to trust myself, and it became easier to let go of the past, to change those stories that were not loving to me. My mantra became, 'If you want a new outcome, you will have to break the habit of being yourself and reinvent a new self.'

Today, I am delighted to be 'dancing with different possibilities'. I am living a life of joy with deep meaningful relationships. My insights included the power of forgiveness, gratitude, and self-love. I am blessed. If you are in that dark place today, remember there is hope and help. Be kind and compassionate to yourself—love yourself. Reach out, then you to will soon be dancing with your different possibilities.

Di Riddell

89

From Toxic to Terrific

*T*he kids used to call me 'druggo' because I had dark circles under my eyes. It hurt me to my core. They were saying there was something wrong with me. I was tested for anemia. It was negative. Through my primary to high school years, I continued to have these dark circles under my eyes as well as bouts of eczema.

I was a social butterfly and wanted to become a beauty therapist. I decided to do my course in Sydney. This soon became my curse and prison. My skin started to break out with pustules, all over my body. Physically, it was horrifically painful. Emotionally, it terrified me because I wanted to start dating. This stopped me dead in my tracks.

I could barely stand the weight of clothes on my skin, let alone makeup. The doctor said it was eczema and announced that I would have it for the rest of my life. At that moment, I felt part of me died. My light grew dark and life seemed over.

At age 21, I was a hermit with no social life and on sleeping tablets daily. I was a slave to my skin, which felt like it had paper cuts all over it. When I woke up, I couldn't move as my skin had seized in the position I had fallen asleep in. It was dreadfully painful physically, debilitating emotionally, and degrading mentally. We tried the doctors one last time, and they told me again it was eczema and that I would have to be hospitalised with cortisone wraps, which was a 'no' from me.

There were times I was so desperate and exhausted to escape the pain that I was at the end of my tether. I realised I knew my body best and I had to start listening to it. As confirmation, the song at the time on the radio was *Tubthumping (I Get Knocked Down)* by Chumbawamba. I used to play this to motivate me. I took action; rather than playing the victim and taking the diagnosis as final, I went to homeopaths and naturopaths who eased the condition. Though I never thought I needed 20 tablets three times a day and eating good food! Intuitively I stopped the tablets but something still wasn't right.

During the years of my health journey, I was interested in a more holistic, spiritual approach to life. I read a lot of articles, saw a lot of healers and experts, and took supplements. I believe they still played a part in supporting me, but the one common thread to my healing was through my food choices. No one else could do this for me. I knew I was suffering from 'sugar shock'. I was a sugar addict.

I decided to heal myself through self-love and empowered wellness. I took my body from acidic to alkaline. I took responsibility and began nurturing my body rather than punishing it. I eliminated sugar, meat, dairy, fake foods, and drinks that cause inflammation in the body and exacerbate conditions. I started to fuel my body with whole foods, cold pressed juices, gentle exercise, chemical-free skin care, and household products.

Very quickly my body, mind, and emotions started to go from toxic to terrific. I could see and feel the benefits of healing myself. My skin cleared up – it was glowing and so soft to touch. The brain fog and headaches stopped. I had more clarity. I felt consistent joy and happiness. My energy was even throughout the day. My breathing improved and I no longer needed medication. I dropped excess weight. I began to sleep through the night and wake feeling refreshed. There are no obsessive cravings. I gained so much more freedom.

I had no idea how liberating it would feel emotionally, physically, and mentally to start living life on a natural high.

Rachel Gascoine

90

Growing Bodacious Self-Love

*J*t was in 2006 that I was beginning an entrepreneurial journey. I was training and learning new skills that contributed to my seeing, for the first time in my life, that anything was possible. Both my partner and I had the vision for an extraordinary life doing extraordinary things: all leading to leaving a legacy around both my family and my favourite projects.

Life was very enjoyable and I felt bulletproof, until one morning during a café meeting, our world came crashing down. We received the news that we were part of a very complex fraud scheme, which relieved us of a serious amount of money.

Over the ensuing months, I felt like I was literally treading water; pulling our very torn life together the best way I could and conjuring up as much of that old 'bulletproof' feeling that I could muster. However, the belief in myself had been severely crushed. What made it even worse was seeing what happened to my amazing partner who took it much worse than I ever realised at the time, and to see him struggle was at times soul-destroying. This is where the very debilitating condition of shame and guilt took over, and whilst on the outside it was though everything was going okay, internally I was in turmoil; full of anger, resentment, frustration, and of course, hurt. I hid this from friends and family to the best of my ability.

It was evident that my ego was in control of me; the stress showed on my face. Worry and doubt also became unwelcome partners. I wasn't a happy being and letting go was incredibly difficult.

It wasn't until I took on the position of vulnerability and embraced the decision to step up and take full responsibility for my life that things changed. I had to adopt a healthy degree of self-love through forgiveness, and crucify the shame, guilt, worry, and doubt that had consumed me for far too long. Only then did I feel a sense of peace begin to reside in my inner being.

This last commitment was the toughest thing I had ever done, but by this stage I was totally fed up with my 'non-life'. I now realised I needed to take a leap of faith and once again embrace my original vision and purpose to create a life of exciting possibilities.

There is a quote that says, 'When something bad happens to you, you have three choices: you either let it define you, let it destroy you, or let it strengthen you.' Taking on the third choice has been both wonderful and revealing. I am being able to laugh at myself and allow myself to be openly vulnerable. I know now that it is a sign of true strength. I feel lighter, and can stand tall and say, 'I made a mistake.' I have learnt to ask better questions and I know that there are people out there who have my back.

I can now laugh at the one thing that I had been so dismissive and afraid of. I have fully immersed myself in the 'process and journey' of learning to live, love, and being vulnerable. This breakthrough has allowed another world to open up, in which for me to stake my claims. I am able to be fully present and extremely grateful that the possibilities and inspiring dreams are manifesting into reality.

To allow myself to be able to dream again has been the crucial step in healing from within. I can now say how truly grateful this life experience has been for me. It has assisted me to have more compassion for those who are walking through tough times in any area and to create a bodacious life.

Jan McIntyre

91

The Gift of Being Different

I realised I was different when I was five.

That's when my sister began digging her nails into my arm and shouting that I was an embarrassment to the family. She told me everyone was laughing at my weird legs and shoes. There were no photos of me at home because I was too ugly.

In some respects, she was right. I was born with my feet twisted so the soles faced up and my legs were bent in half bringing my feet to the inside of both thighs.

Casts on both legs straightened my legs and, until I started walking, my feet were encased in rigid shoes fastened to a steel bar to keep them in the correct anatomical positions. As I grew, the external evidence of my problems reduced to knock knees and orthopaedic shoes. The emotional damage was more persistent.

I felt worthless after years of taunts and bullying from my sister and classmates. I pretended to be sick to avoid school and cried wondering why people couldn't see past the external things to get to know me. I felt trapped in an existence I couldn't escape from and prayed for a solution.

My life changed when I was 15 and a 'friend' invited me to cheerleading practice saying I'd have fun and would easily learn the moves. I was so happy to be included with the cool kids that it never occurred to me it was a set-up. When I realised it was the final try-out for the team, it was too late to back out and my performance was a failure. The 'friend' stood at the side laughing with the other girls.

Usually, I would have bowed my head and left. But a strength and conviction I'd never felt before overcame me. I'd had enough. I thought about how lucky I was to be able to walk. And the wisdom of a phrase my father said to me every day finally sunk in, 'Be a leader, not a follower, and don't let anyone tell you what to do.' I wish I'd told him before he died how much those simple words have guided me in life.

That day liberated me.

I started what are now called visualisation techniques but what for me were images of being successful, liked and helping others. I thanked my birth defects for being the gift that helped me develop a deep empathy and compassion for people. For the first time in my life, I learnt what confidence felt like.

That confidence has rarely left and has helped me start several international businesses where my focus was on developing customer relationships. My specialty was working with critical and judgemental people. After all, I've had plenty of experience with this!

I'd like to say life has been easy since that day at 15, but growth is an ongoing process. Accepting yourself for who you are is one of the kindest things you will do for yourself. It's also beneficial for your health. Having a positive outlook reduces stress and boosts confidence. It increases the levels of the brain's 'feel good' chemicals and helps your heart.

Consider your differences as a gift to you, your friends, and family. Never underestimate the impact you will have on someone's life by getting to really know them and showing them the power of being comfortable as yourself. Believe that you were born the way you were for a purpose. Know that you are enough.

Cindy Galvin

92

Healing from Beyond the Veil

"*T*hank you, I love you." I waited 60 years for those words from my father – to hear them and to say them to him. And that touch – that touch I had known in childhood that somehow disappeared as I grew to become a man. That touch that said in its own way, 'Thank you, I love you.' I had sought for years to find the way to say those words and to find that touch – but despite so wanting to, I somehow couldn't.

The moment for which I had been preparing over the previous five years showed up. It fell to me to say to him, 'There is nothing now that can be done.' And then, in the moments that followed the abject terror I saw in his eyes, he stilled and his eyes held mine with an timeless ferocity of gaze and attention. Only then did I know how great a man he was. My heart burst asunder as quite another force took over and everything else in my life fell into insignificance for presence to reign.

The removing of the monitors, the clips and the attachments were unnoticed by him as he navigated his final hours, breath by breath, heartbeat by heartbeat. It was so profound, so unutterably final and stark. Then came the final goodbye: the handing over to the ultimate mystery of death, to God and to life.

But that was but the beginning of the journey to those words and that touch. Craving time to be alone with this giant of a man, this father of mine. The comings and goings of the hours that followed meant those moments came only when his last breath had been drawn – that moment of indescribable beauty, of poignant finality, of the stupendous unknown. And there, in the stillness of the stark bare hospital room, cold, with a howling gale and driving rain outside as the grey morning light crept in. The space became a sacred temple to the worship and adoration of this beautiful man and his life.

There in that portal to the everlasting, I could lay my head on his chest and hold him. In that deep silence, we talked the talk that could never before be shared. Pouring my heart out in breath-taking simplicity, he heard me and received me. There in that aloneness with this great man whose courage floored and awed me, he spoke to me from a space beyond time.

In full resonance, his once irradiated voice now healed to tell me he could see now what it is that I have been doing all these years, and now knowing, he wanted to give me his blessing to go and do what I am doing. To keep going, to know I am on the right track and that all is well and always will be. "Thank you, I love you," he said in the silence of that sacred moment. 'Thank you, I love you – go on your way, now I can see.'

Those words, those sounds, went beyond healing, beyond anything I had known. Those moments were the culmination of both of our lives – father to son and son to father. Hallowed in name; the Kingdom came. Everything changed – yet nothing changed – everything, absolutely everything.

And now it is my turn for the family of Man, to stand on his shoulders and keep going – to love and be loved – to heal and be healed. Beyond forgiveness, as far beyond forgiveness as the mind can conceive, is love made manifest in the state of grace those words inspire and create. With all my heart and mind and soul I pray, 'Thank you, I love you.'

Dr. Kim Jobst

93

Believe In Your Value

For years, I had a reoccurring cycle where I would feel disrespected, devalued, annoyed, and even disappointed. I would dust it all off, tell myself things will be better. I pretended I was ok.

A year of situations slapping me in the face around devaluing myself, which brought up anger, frustration, and stress. In that was the moment I chose to STOP EVERYTHING. No longer could I pretend to myself. I decided to fall into the depths of whatever this reoccurring pattern was. I had been waiting to be acknowledged, appreciated, and valued; I was hoping doors would open, so I could share my work with a bigger audience, yet I was being shut down all the time.

The straw that broke my spirit was when I reached out to a person who suggested that I was 'overreacting'. I knew the only option was to follow the energy to the core of this pattern. It was my healing journey and an absolute act of self-love to finally face it. It wasn't pretty, easy or pleasant, as I faced the lies I had lived and the untruths I told myself to keep me showing up in life.

Disconnecting from everything and becoming a 'cave dweller' meant I had to be with myself. I still functioned in life; however, I was quieter, less available. I actually gifted myself the time to heal, and funny enough, when we do this the universe supports us in so many ways.

Each day I would ask myself', 'What am I lying to myself about?' As that question would move through me, pathways from my subconscious would deliver 'lies' into my consciousness. In those moments I had the opportunity to change the old lie, to my new truth. Simple! Maybe, but confronting on so many levels. Getting real with ourselves is healing; awareness is healing; self-responsibility is healing.

One morning after doing this for a number of weeks, I was in the state between sleep and awareness and I saw it: the big lie. In my mind's eye, there was a rock and carved into were the words, 'Whatever you do on your own, you will flop.' It was instant. That was the moment where life shifts gears in expanded awareness. My ONLY thought and response was fierce, 'That is a lie, it is NOT me.' As I stated that, I put in place the belief that is true for me NOW.

As I witnessed the rock crumble into tiny particles and dissolve, I heard the voice of the person who had made that statement many years ago and I had taken it as true. It was underneath so many things in my life; devaluing anything I was attempting to achieve, grow through or expand into. I believed I had no value in myself!

As a deep belief, it affected everything. Seeking validation became a silent cry for approval and acceptance. No more! The next step was to find my own value through my own acknowledgement within. Having found the core issue, I needed to know the next step. It was instantly received via a 'spiritual message' giving me a deep inner knowing.

Today, I value myself and all that I am. I am willing and prepared to do what it takes to express myself. That daily declaration aligned me to my own self-value. From the moment I started to say this as a command, my energy field shifted. Within days, doors shut for years opened. Invitations and opportunities arrived; things I had wanted to participate in were now looking for me.

Instead of wanting others to value me, I valued myself completely and life changed dramatically. The pattern has never repeated as I dealt with the core issue; I followed the energy to the heart and sat in it for months.

Raelene Byrne

94

Be Limitless

Surfing was my world. I lived and worked to surf. When I was on my board I felt complete and balanced – at one with the world. It felt like I was home. On November 22, 2007, I woke at the usual time, 5:00a.m. I heard the rain on the roof. After having breakfast and packing my lunch, I made a quick dash to my ute. I drove slowly down the highway, barely able to see in front of me with the rain coming down in buckets. Exiting the highway, the ute began aquaplaning. I corrected a couple of times before I decided to rejoin the highway. However, it turned out that I was too late and collided with another car with my head hitting the steering wheel.

The emergency services arrived and quickly cut me out. I was rushed to Nambour General Hospital before being transferred to the Princess Alexandra Hospital in Brisbane. There, I was taken to intensive care, where I was put into an induced coma. I also had a fracture to the pelvis and had bruises and bleeding in my brain.

Seven days later, I woke up from the coma with a lot of people around me but no conscious recollection of who they were. I was suffering from short-term memory loss (Post Traumatic Amnesia). It would be two weeks before I gradually began to recognise my family and friends. As I started to heal and become more stable, I was transferred back to Nambour until I checked out on Christmas Day. I returned to the PA Brain Injury Rehabilitation Unit and started physiotherapy, occupational therapy and speech pathology.

I had to re-learn everything. Learn to walk, talk and communicate, just as a small child learns for the first time. The doctor told me that I would never be able to do anything with my life. I was in hospital on the weekdays and with my family on weekends. We spent a lot of time at the beach, though, frustratingly as I wasn't yet allowed to surf. My brain injury meant I could only swim and sit on the beach.

After a time, I started to get quite pissed off. I was spending more time at the hospital than I was at the beach and still not allowed to surf. It felt like I was not allowed to do anything. I decided that this was not how I wanted my life to be. I was not going to play by the rules of other people. I wanted to live a more authentic version of myself and creatively express who I was.

After one of my talks with my dad, I saw that I had to come forward and be present. I needed to focus on building my self-worth. I took responsibility for my life and became responsible for me expanding my mind, body and consciousness. I used surfing as a tool to give back to myself.

I decided to heal my body with the understanding that through pain there is greatness. So once I was given the all clear to surf, I used that time on the waves to be at one with the ocean and allow my body to heal itself. It was my meditation.

So, it was through persistence and seeing outcomes that I wanted for myself, and which weren't the opinion of others, that I returned to full health. I'm here to live my dream, to leave my mark on this world. In doing so, I have decided that people can be a part of my life and I can listen to what they say but I don't have to do what they say. I'm not going to let other people set my limits. That is for me to do for myself.

Leroy Midgley

95

Responsibility for Oneself

"*I*f you were 80 years of age, the number of lesions on your brain and spine would be normal."

The doctor said, in 2012. I was 31 years old. Fear and relief pervaded me. Fear that I wasn't exactly sure what Multiple Sclerosis was, and how it would affect me; and relief that I finally had a name to put on the symptoms I was experiencing.

I entered hospital for steroid treatment to shrink the lesion on my spine. I spent the majority of my time comforting everyone who was worried about me telling them I was FINE. I didn't want pity; I didn't want to accept this was really happening, so I dug a great big hole in the sand and firmly placed my head in it. Funnily enough, this strategy didn't work out so well. The next four years were spent fighting my way through what can only be described as a very dark period.

Sick, fat, tired, and angry is a good description. I spent the majority of my 'feeling good' time at work. I arrived home reluctantly to take injections. I suffered fevers, nausea, flu symptoms and pure exhaustion. I merely existed. To an outsider, I was happy, bright, and positive; yet I had such inner turmoil. I was trying to keep up a façade of being okay, because I actually couldn't admit to myself I wasn't.

Every twitch, pain, ounce of fatigue sent my body and mind into panic wondering if this was another attack – if it was MS striking again. Debilitating anxiety would wash over me playing out every possible negative scenario.

Something had to give. December 2014 came along, and I decided to give up the only identity I was proud of: my job as a Media Sales & Marketing Manager. I had to try something different.

I could no longer cope with the side effects of the medication, so I stopped taking all of it against the wishes of my neurologist and family.

Staying at home with my kids should have been a joy, but I resented giving up my career and relying on someone else financially.

In January 2016, I attended a Tony Robbins seminar after begging every contact for a free ticket. My friend Brendan secured one for me 30 minutes before the event.

The talk had such a profound effect on me. I can safely say it was the biggest turn around in life I ever could have wished for at precisely the right time. I realised I needed to take accountability and responsibility for myself. I made a decision that very day that I was going to cure myself as well as be happy no matter what I had to do.

I started to put myself first, unapologetically. I said no to people or events I didn't feel were in my best interests; even cutting out some gossipy friends and generally anyone negative. I practised meditation even more and gratitude. I invested in personal development and most importantly, faced my inner demons.

The results were astounding, as soon as I started respecting myself, my body started to mirror that. I felt like a better person, I was at peace and my body and illness finally followed suit. 'Whatever you have been doing, keep doing it,' were the words of my neurologist in January 2017.

I now dedicate my time helping people realise their full potential choosing the life they want to live.

Karen Dwyer

96

So My Story Begins

O n my 15th birthday, a wave of darkness came over me, which was later labelled as 'clinical depression'. At 21, I had a number of emotionally traumatic events happen, including a 'bad trip' on ecstasy, which put me into a psychosis. Alongside this, I also developed anxiety. The anxiety was exhausting and after about a year, I went into adrenal burnout which developed into neurological symptoms. I experienced fatigue, fluctuating weakness, and reduced sensation through the right side of my body.

I saw physicians and specialists and had many investigations, none of which ever came back conclusive of any physical related illness or disease. So, I was given the label of 'chronic fatigue'. I went from healthy and fit – able to run 10 km a day – to barely being able to walk 100 metres. I felt like I was on a constant emotional roller coaster. Because I felt so anxious all of the time, I began withdrawing from people and barely leaving the house. When people asked me how I was, I pretended everything was okay and told them I was 'fine'.

That was until one night about a year later. Laying in the bath at my dad's apartment, I noticed that I was starting to have suicidal thoughts. It was in that moment that I knew I had to change the trajectory of my life, which was petrifying, as I had no idea where to start.

I was raised as an atheist who always challenged my religious education teacher. Beyond all of the ideas and beliefs I had grown up with about religion 'being a load of bullshit' (as my mum would say), I had a deep knowing during the middle of my crisis that I needed to pray. And so I did. I placed my hands together and raised them above my head, crying as I asked for help, 'If there is something bigger than myself, please show me some sign that everything is going to be okay.'

And in that moment, I had a vision. I was standing at the gates of a monastery. It was just a flash, nothing more, but I had never had any clear visions like that before. After a series of synchronistic events, six months later I found myself standing at those exact monastery gates. That was the beginning of my journey of opening myself up to a connection with a power much greater than myself.

Ever since, I have been divinely guided by a mysterious force that I didn't care to name. Recently, my inner guidance led me to trying Kambo, a sacred medicine that comes from the secretion of the giant monkey tree frog from the Amazon.

I sat in ceremony with the medicine twice in one month: once on the full and then on the following new moon. The first time I took the medicine, after about 15 minutes, I felt heat start to come up through my right leg, and then after a few minutes, it went numb. When the effects of the Kambo wore off a few hours later, I had complete sensation back within the right side of my body. This was the first time in five years that the left and right side of my body felt the same.

Ever since taking the medicine, the neurological symptoms I experienced have been completely healed. I am now back at the gym and able to do high intensity workouts, something that I couldn't tolerate before because of the high levels of fatigue and weakness I was experiencing. My emotions have been more stable and I have had very little anxiety, something that I used to experience quite regularly.

I am so blessed and grateful for my journey with this medicine and to be able to share my story of healing with others.

Sigourney Belle Weldon

97

Healing Cancer Naturally

"We have the results of the biopsy, and I can tell you the tissue samples did test positive for cancer." I'd been expecting this diagnosis ever since the biopsy six days before. The consultant had been very clear about her expectation; until now, there was always the possibility that the lump could be something benign. Not so.

It was a strange and disorienting time, and it took me a few days to recover myself enough to want to engage with the world. Yet, somehow, I seemed to sense pretty quickly there were things I could do to help myself. I contacted my homeopath after the biopsy, and stopped taking my hormone replacement therapy (HRT) that same day after a chat with my GP. Within days of the diagnosis being confirmed, my husband, Dyfrig, and I learned what we could about cancer, its causes, and how it develops. We adopted a predominantly plant-based diet.

I'd known, intellectually, that the chances of getting cancer were around one in three, but because I'd thought it would never happen to me, the idea of prevention hadn't seriously entered my head. That meant I hadn't educated myself about lifestyle choices that could tip the odds more in my favour, and I was completely ignorant of just how much I could do to improve my own outcome.

When faced with the shock of a biopsy-proven diagnosis, education became an urgent priority. What I discovered astounded me; and led to a major transformation in my life. My healing journey really began as soon as I started educating myself. I was astonished to discover a number of non-toxic healing therapies, beyond the traditional treatments of surgery, chemotherapy, and radiation. I discovered a range of foods and natural substances, such as turmeric, that has many health benefits that could support me in recovering my health.

Alongside this education came a rational assessment of the pros and cons of orthodox treatment. The standard approach I was being offered would weaken my immune system. It could possibly increase the likelihood of cancer recurring elsewhere in my body in future years, since research suggests chemo and radiotherapy are both carcinogenic in their own right. It would also require me to take pharmaceutical drugs for several years subsequently, with a host of possible side effects.

Many people had healed themselves from cancer using non-toxic approaches, including those who'd been told by their doctors there was nothing more they could do. Also as a result of my research came the realisation that cancer wasn't something that had happened to me out of the blue. It wasn't some malevolent alien growing inside me but, rather, something generated by my own body. It was my body's natural response to conditions I had unknowingly created. And if I had caused this, then I could un-cause it.

During the months following the diagnosis, I acted on what I learnt by adopting a hardcore nutritional protocol and multiple non-toxic therapies. Monthly ultrasounds showed rapid shrinkage beyond what would have been expected from chemo, leaving only scar tissue within three months; a result described as 'remarkable' by one of the integrative doctors I consulted.

Cancer had shifted me from being a pill-popping workaholic running on energy drinks, to someone who was effectively healed; and in better health than I had been for the previous 20 years with a new outlook on life. Unlikely as it may have seemed back then, diagnosis proved to be one of my life's greatest gifts.

Debra White Hughes

98

Loving My Life Again

When I was in school, I was a bright and intelligent kid, popular among all. I was exceptionally good in my studies and I won trophies for the school whenever I took part in literary competitions. I used to take part in public debates and speech contests. Since day one, I never tasted a single defeat. Winning had become my thing and it was engraved, not only in my mind, but in the minds of my parents who also thought that I was born to win and I could never touch rock bottom.

One time on stage during a contest, I stuttered and forgot what to say next. I saw people staring at me and I felt scared and was unable to breathe for a millionth part of second. When the result was out, I had lost a very important state level competition. It was my first time dealing with stuttering, fear of public speaking and panic attacks, and my last time speaking in front of people on any stage without losing it.

For everyone around me, it was not a big deal to lose, but to me, it felt like losing all my courage and confidence, and was the start of an emotionally wrecked journey. I was battling with my self-esteem, panic attacks (which at that time was considered asthma attacks) and my fear of public speaking. I was still a good student and a good friend. People would come to me and talk, but as soon as I had a panic attack, mostly everyone would slowly walk away, thinking that I have some sort of 'djinn' or supernatural creatures attacking me and I would haunt them too. Some of my fellows said that it is my social drama to seek attention.

The worst battle was this social battle, a social label. At home, my worried parents would take me to a physician to cure my asthma, but not to a therapist. First, we did not know about panic attacks. Second, going to a therapist is a kind of public announcement of you becoming a complete lunatic.

Whenever I sat alone and thought about my future, everything seemed dark and blurry. Sometimes I would think of it as my own fault, sometimes I would shout at my parents, assuming I was a victim of 'djinn', and there were times when I would just sit in tears at night thinking about ill treatment of others and eventually developing a far lower self-esteem.

On one of those days, I looked at the sky with a hope of getting my answers and with an urge to change my reality; I saw clouds covering the sun and the sun lightening up the linings of those clouds.

Something hit me hard, the beauty of nature and the power of being granted to everything in it. As Richard Bach said, in *Jonathan Livingston Seagull*, 'To fly as fast as thought, you must begin by knowing that you have already arrived.'

I realised that there is more to see in me, and I found my strength. I realised that I already had everything I needed for fighting the social and individual battles, and I can change my mindset as well. I started accepting every challenge with a core belief that I can overcome it, and I did, too.

Voila, months have passed without having panic attacks or recurrent hospital visits. I have successfully removed my social label as well.

Laraib Fatima Malik

99

Five Dollars

My story begins in a small country town in rural South Australia. When I say 'small', I do really mean small. The town only has a hall, a general store, a mechanic and – lest I forget – a phone box. I lived with my family on a sheep and grain farm about 6 km from town and 150 km from the city of Adelaide. My childhood was normal, I guess. Like most kids, we got teased, played with friends, did Scouts and local sport.

I remember the day my dad had his heart attack. It didn't kill him, but we had to sell the farm and move to the seaside town of Victor Harbor. I lived there till I was 12. It was there I finished years ten through 12. I did alright at school, I was taught to get good grades, get a good job, and work until retirement.

That seemed like a plan. Unfortunately, I started to do exactly that, I became a perfect product of the system. I had worked hard at many jobs until I found work as a jewellery finisher in a mass production factory.

I worked my way through the factory until I was a supervisor in the stone setting department. I had remembered my grandfather speaking about working his fingers to the bone, but never really understood the term until I got that job. You see, using emery paper on your fingers takes off all your skin on your fingertips until they bleed. Then came the worst week, the fingers were just the start. That week, I found my girlfriend cheating on me, my grandfather passed away, I hated my job, I had two Visa cards maxed out and I was on my last five dollars.

I needed fuel to get home, so I pulled into the local fuel station and the only money I could find was five dollars in coins in the car's ashtray. So, I put exactly five dollars of fuel into the car, and walked into the service station with coins covered in apple cinnamon scented dust from the ashtray. I felt so incredibly small, like such a failure and totally judged by the people behind me.

As I left the counter, I just wanted the ground to swallow me whole. I didn't care if I lived or died. Who would miss me after all? As I walked back to the car, my dream car pulled into the station, a beautiful 1978 V8 metallic blue Ford Coupe. I cursed God, 'Why don't you just rub my nose in it?' As I walked around the car the owner opened his door and pulled his wheelchair across his lap and placed it next to the car. It then hit me like a ton of bricks.

I realised I didn't know that guy or how he came to be in a wheelchair, I am guessing it wasn't his fault. It made me realise that I was the total sum of all the decisions I had made. I went out with that girl and took that job and those two maxed out Visa cards. I realised that I was okay, and that I could change.

I studied business and opened my own manufacturing jewellery business - my first. I ran it for five years before I opened my second company. In the second year of opening SA Gold Traders, my wife and I turned over $3.2 million in business. I am not saying this to impress you, I am saying it to press upon you that anyone can make it. I just didn't listen to the people who told me I couldn't.

My passion now is to teach men and women in business to keep their marriages together.

Lee Chapman

100

Reclaiming My Sleep

*J*n 2012, I was working six days a week selling books. I loved my job. Without any notice, the company went into liquidation and I suddenly found myself unemployed and unemployable; as it turned out as no one wanted to hire someone over 60. So, feeling like I had no other option, I retired.

After several weeks, I began to notice that I felt tired when I woke up and couldn't work a full day without resting: a stark contrast to the ten-hour days I had effortlessly worked just weeks earlier. Over the next 12 months as I felt more and more tired, I began having a sleep during the day. Sometimes as early as 10.00 a.m. Because I was so exhausted, I lacked the motivation to do anything. I felt like a zombie and that life was passing me by.

I couldn't see a reason for my being so tired. At the time. I was eating well and exercising, and, up until I was let go from my job, my sleep had been deep. The only thing that had changed was that I was no longer working. After a year of frustration, my life felt like a train wreck.

Driving home from the airport early one morning, I momentarily fell asleep at the wheel doing 80 kph. When I 'woke' up, I was heading towards the tunnel wall. Having almost killed myself from my tiredness, I knew I needed to see a doctor that day. He referred me to a clinic to have my sleep patterns monitored.

The test revealed that I was waking 85 times an hour. In other words, I had chronic sleep apnoea where you stop breathing in your sleep (people die because of it). Now it made sense why I was fatigued every day. The solution? Be hooked up to a machine to keep my airways open for the rest of my life. No way, José!

I knew it was time for a drastic change. So, I began to reflect on where my life was so out of alignment that it was costing me my sleep. I decided my first step was to keep my mouth closed while sleeping. I came up with a genius idea to stretch a girl's headband over my face from chin to crown, thus forcing myself to breathe through my nose (luckily there are no photos of this!) It was silly, but it worked as a temporary solution while I addressed the underlying emotional issue.

I read in Inna Segal's book, *The Secret Language of Your Body*, that the emotion behind sleep apnoea is not trusting in life. WOW. It suddenly became clear to me that I had been plagued by worry about my future ever since I had stopped working: Where was the money going to come from? How would I survive? Would I be okay?

I felt I had to be in control of my life, and while you can do this to an extent during the day, it's a different matter at night as sleeping requires you to let go in order to relax. Hence, I was waking 85 times an hour to check that everything was okay.

The illusion I had in all of this was that I had control of my life during the day. When I realised how little control I actually had over many things including people, the weather, drivers on the road, and even my body, my need to know everything all the time dissolved completely. I felt safe again.

After a week, the sleep apnoea disappeared. I knew it had gone because I was dreaming again!

I had reclaimed my zzzzzzzz's.

Rae Antony

101

The Healing Power of Writing

Writing has been part of my life since before I was born. My mother read to me for over 400 hours in the womb before I even made my entrance into the world. And so, it's no surprise to me that words have followed me through my life, or that writing stirs a deep feeling of unconditional love: like being held and supported by my mother when I was in the womb.

I wrote throughout my childhood, mostly fictional stories about puppy dogs and kittens going on holidays to tropical islands (I also recall writing a small book about my budgerigar that died when I was eight). But when I reached my teenage years, my world changed forever — and so did my relationship with writing.

I had moved from a primary school of 24 students to a high school of nearly a thousand students. I developed anxiety as I tried to navigate my way through the ocean of students who were taller, cooler, and more popular than me. I felt small, insignificant, unattractive, and lost; I certainly didn't feel like my voice mattered. How could it, in such a big crowd? I was a minnow in a very large pond, and I spent most days feeling socially excluded.

Adolescent hormones had kicked in and my emotions were deep and confusing. It seemed that no one understood me, not even my parents. Outside of the classes — which I both enjoyed and excelled in — it didn't seem to matter whether I existed. After my first love broke up with me at age 14, I fell apart and contemplated the idea of ending my life.

One Friday night, I was sitting in front of the computer. I'd had a rough week and being alone brought relief. Something stirred within me and I opened a Word document. In ten minutes, I wrote a poem that captured how I was feeling (I recall it beginning with the phrase, 'You could cut the tension with a knife'). Suddenly, my angst and pain were no longer trapped inside me. They were free on the page and I was free, too. I had found healing.

In the year that I was 14, I wrote 170 poems and short pieces. I collated them into a book – a ring binder – and printed several copies. I gave them to the few friends I had and my teachers. While my teachers were concerned about my emotional wellbeing, due to how dark my writing was, my friends were moved. One girlfriend said, "I read this at night before I go to sleep and it helps me." I'm not sure exactly what drove me to share my writing, but I do know that it changed my life forever.

It was then that I realised that my writing not only had the power to heal me, it could heal others, too. Fast-forward to today, I have more than nine published books. I have written millions of words on the topic of living your dreams. I have built a thriving career sharing my innermost thoughts, feelings, and knowledge with the world. I'm certain there are many, many more messages waiting to emerge from within me onto the page.

I don't know where I would be without my writing – or if I would be here at all. My writing has not only healed me from the inside out, but it has led me to the life of my dreams. And had it not been for the angst I experienced as a teenager, I'm not sure I would have stumbled onto the path of my inspired destiny. And for that, I have no words.

Emily Gowor

Contact the Authors

We highly recommend that you reach out and connect with the authors who have contributed their stories to this book.

Story	Author Name	Website
1	Carmen Braga	http://www.healingheartscentre.ca
2	Amanda Rodd	https://www.instagram.com/amanda.rodd/
3	Leonie Lancaster	
4	Karen Reys	www.ceedhealings.com
5	Bridget Wood	http://www.bridgetwood.net/
6	Shona Blackthorn	http://tamarhypnotherapy.weebly.com
7	Daniel Lyttle	www.DanielLyttle.com
8	Louise Cramond	http://www.soulmumma.com
9	Billy Flett	www.billyflett.com
10	Sue McKenna	http://www.happybreastbalm.com/
11	Kate Moloney	kate@katemoloney.com
12	Helen Travers	http://www.aboutme.helen.travers
13	Ayla Saylik	
14	Ana Palacios de las Casas	http://anapalacios.org
15	Anthony Hudson	http://www.anthonyhudson.com.au
16	Irene Treacy	www.smoveyhealth.com
17	Estelita Pearce	https://www.estelitapearcewellness.com
18	Deborah Stathis	http://www.tragicopportunities.com
19	Heather Joy Bassett	http://heatherjoybassett.com
20	Joshua McNess	http://www.joshuamcness.com
21	Emme Krystelle	https://about.me/emme.k
22	Delwyn Webb	http://www.linkedin.com/in/delwyn-webb-302766160

23	Tami Jane	http://innerconnect.com.au/about/
24	Alison Morris	http://www.alisonmorris.com.au
25	Jo Tocher	http://www.life-after-miscarriage.com
26	Lance Garbutt	http://lanceg6.wixsite.com/neverendingjourney
27	Dr. Marcia Becherel	www.drmarciabecherel.com
28	Maria Solano	http://heartsoulhealth.wordpress.com/about/
29	Dannii Orawiec	http://www.danniiorawiec.com
30	Carolynne Melnyk	http://www.livinglifeinjoy.com
31	Stephan Gardner	http://www.stephangardner.com
32	Jason Russell	www.russfit.com.au
33	Jeani Howard	http://www.everychance.net
34	Andrea Baumann	http://www.andreabaumann.com
35	Jeff Withers	http://www.lovedynamics.global
36	Fiona Hurle	http://www.fionahurle.com
37	Sheila Kennedy	http://www.sheila-kennedy.com
38	Carolina Rotaru	www.carolinarotaruphotography.com
39	Naveen Light	http://www.kokizen.com/
40	Dave Tuck	www.SupremeWellnessCoaching.com
41	Elina Passant	http://www.justsoelina.com
42	Heather Passant	http://www.lifeharmony.com.au
43	Delvina Waiti	http://about.me/delvinawaiti
44	Jo Worthy	http://www.joworthy.com
45	Vas Bes	https://vasbes.wixsite.com/selflovesuccess
46	Shaune Clarke	www.bigbrandspeaking.com
47	Jennie de Vine	http://Universalreiki.com.au
48	Michelle Walker	http://www.michellewalker.com.au/
49	Helga Dalla	http://about.me/helgadalla
50	Elysia Anketell	www.thebodylovecollective.com
51	Jackie Mortimer	http://angelsofintelligence.com

52	Nicole Taryn	http://nicoletaryn.com
53	Christine Di Leone	Christine Dileone
54	Rachel Saliba	http://www.practicallylearning.com.au
55	Nick Condon	http://breakthrough-adventurer.com
56	Franca Mazzarella	http://www.infinitedreamcoaching.com.au
57	Anne Namakando Phiri	
58	Hilary Cave	www.hilarycave.com
59	Robert J Grimes	http://robertjgrimes.com.au
60	Hayley Scott	http://www.hayleyscott.com.au
61	Slava Komzic	www.slavakomzik.com
62	Tony Brown	http://www.squidpublishing.com/
63	Sabrina Souto	www.fertileway.com
64	Kim Guthrie	http://www.workingonwellness.com.au/
65	Shane Breslin	http://www.shanebreslin.com/
66	Sally Moore	http://www.sallymoorelifecoach.com.au
67	Maree Malouf	http://www.lovedynamics.global
68	Cat McRad	http://www.singtoself.com
69	Katina Cuba	http://www.expandegroup.com
70	Tony Inman	http://www.tonyinman.com.au
71	Jo Trewartha	http://www.freeyourmindsolutions.com
72	Carlosifus Holden	https://www.instagram.com/carlosifus/
73	Hazel Butterworth	http://www.HealingHeartsCentre.ca
74	Luanne Mareen	www.GoddessonPurpose.com
75	Angela Peris	www.cardiacwellness.com.au
76	Natasha Jones	http://beautifulpowerfulyou.net
77	Alan Jackson	www.amped.life
78	Faye Rushton	www.fayerushton.com
79	Dr. Olivier Becherel	https://masterytosuccess.com.au

80	Jaswinder Challi Sahiba	http://www.jaz-nur.com
81	Panayiota	www.panayiota.com.au
82	Kim Knight	https://www.emotionalalchemyacademy.com
83	Sharyn Bailey	http://about.me/sharynbailey
84	Faye Waterman	http://www.fayewaterman.com.au
85	Deborah Toussaint	http://deborahtoussaint.com
86	George Masempela	www.istillcallzambiahome.com
87	Manmeet Chowdhry	http://www.manmeetchowdhry.com
88	Di Riddell	http://www.diriddell.com
89	Rachel Gascoine	http://about.me/rachelgascoine
90	Jan McIntyre	http://about.me/JanMcIntyre
91	Cindy Galvin	http://www.cindygalvin.com
92	Dr. Kim Jobst	www.functionalshift.com
93	Raelene Byrne	http://raelenebyrne.com/
94	Leroy Midgley	www.leroyssurfschool.com
95	Karen Dwyer	http://www.mstosuccess.com/
96	Sigourney Weldon	www.sigourneybelle.com
97	Debra White Hughes	www.consciouslycreatinghealth.com
98	Laraib Malik	http://www.instagram.com/laa_raibb
99	Lee Chapman	http://www.mrleechapman.com/
100	Rae Antony	www.mamaraessoulfood.com/
101	Emily Gowor	http://www.emilygowor.com

Recommended Reading

- *The Body Is the Barometer of the Soul* – Annette Noontil
- *The Secret Language of Your Body* – Inna Segal
- *You Can Heal Your Life* – Louise Hay
- *Breaking the Habit of Being Yourself* – Dr. Joe Dispenza
- *The Biology of Belief* – Bruce Lipton
- *The Power of Intention* – Wayne Dyer
- *The Breakthrough Experience* – Dr. John Demartini
- *The Journey* – Brandon Bays

Acknowledgments

$\mathcal{J}$ would love to show my gratitude to the following people for their contribution in bringing this book to life.

Firstly, to Rae Antony for having the courage to share her story of healing sleep apnoea on social media in the middle of 2017, and to Carmen Braga for responding to Rae's story to suggest that we combine healing stories together into a book. It is because of your huge hearts and creativity that this book is in people's hands today; I love you both.

I would also love to thank and acknowledge the 101 contributors – including myself and Rae Antony – who chose to step forward and boldly share their stories as part of this book. These stories are an example of what is possible once we look within for the answers. You have shown other people that there is hope in our darkest moments. Thank you for contributing to this book: you have fulfilled our original vision beyond my initial hopes.

My gratitude extends again to Rae Antony for her tireless work in helping the contributors finalise and edit their stories for the book. Your devotion inspires me daily. My acknowledgement also extends to the production team from Gowor International Publishing, who turned this book from a first manuscript into a finished product.

About Emily Gowor

*E*mily Gowor is an inspirational writer, author, and speaker.

After overcoming depression at age 19, Emily devoted herself and her life to bringing writing and inspiration to the world – and she has now spent more than a decade showing people that it is possible to live an extraordinary life.

As the author of more than nine published books on the topics of self-help, entrepreneurship and writing – including *The Book Within You* and *The Inspirational Messenger* – Emily produced an award-winning blog, *Life Travels* in 2010 and 2011, attracting thousands of readers. Emily worked with Dr. John Demartini on his international best-selling book *Inspired Destiny* in 2009 and shared the stage with him in Melbourne, Australia in 2015.

Emily's writings, projects and speaking presentations have touched and moved thousands globally as she inspires people to reach for more. Her purpose-finding tool, the *Inspiration Formula*, is licensed to consultants around the world who are dedicated to showing clients a lasting glimpse of their destiny on Earth. As a winner of the 2012 and 2014 *Anthill 30under30 Young Entrepreneur Award,* Emily has been featured in a range of media sharing her inspirational messages.

Having fulfilled upon a profound and thriving career in her 20s, Emily finds continual inspiration in the world as she continues to bring her love for humanity to the forefront into all she does.

www.emilygowor.com

About Rae Antony

*M*ama Rae is an accomplished gluten, dairy, and refined sugar free food artist, cooking food with heaven in every bite that changes people's perception of what food tastes like.

With almost 60 years experience together with the knowledge she has learned along the way, Mama Rae has developed her unique style that tantalises the taste buds of the fussiest of eaters. The most important ingredient Mama Rae uses in all her recipes is love. That and her love of people means her cooking has changed people's lives as well as their digestion in as little as one week.

Mama Rae caters for events as well as teaches people how to cook simple nutritious and delicious food through her e-kitchen.

'I immediately felt the health benefits of Mama Rae's food! I felt energised after every meal. I loved all of the food she cooked. When you watch Mama Rae at work in the kitchen, you can see the love being added to the food throughout the process. The food comes to life when she laughs! Magic in action before your eyes!'

Mama Rae believes that by giving every thought love and gratitude from deciding what to cook, through to washing the dishes, people will taste your love in the meal you have shared with them.

www.mamaraessoulfood.com

Printed in Australia
AUHW010802211119
320273AU00002B/2

9 780648 588528